A Diary of
DREAMS
AND
VISIONS

A Diary of DREAMS AND VISIONS

Discovering God's Love In The Secret Place

DARREN HIBBS

10 WEEK BOOKS
10WeekBooks.com

A DIARY OF DREAMS AND VISIONS

Copyright © 2013 Darren Hibbs
Published by 10 Week Books

All rights reserved.

Scriptures taken from the Holy Bible, New International Version®, NIV®. Copyright © 1973, 1978, 1984, 2011 by Biblica, Inc.™ Used by permission of Zondervan. All rights reserved worldwide. www.zondervan.com The "NIV" and "New International Version" are trademarks registered in the United States Patent and Trademark Office by Biblica, Inc.™

ISBN: 0988919559
ISBN-13:   978-0-9889195-5-6

No part of this book may be reproduced in any form or by any electronic or mechanical means including information storage and retrieval systems, without permission in writing from the author. The only exception is by a reviewer, who may quote short excerpts in a review.

10 WEEK BOOKS

10WeekBooks.com

Printed in the United States
10 9 8 7 6 5 4 3 2 1

This collection of short stories is dedicated to all those who came before me and encouraged me to go deeper in God's love by sharing their stories.

Contents

Acknowledgements i

Preface iii

1 A Diary 1

2 The People God Loves 8

3 Raising The Dead 14

4 Growing In The Prophetic 24

5 A Brother's Dream 38

6 September 11, 2001 48

7 Prophets 64

8 Jesus, A Hot Dog And A Coke 78

9 The Most Helpful Gift 86

Sample Now The Good News 100

About The Author 114

Other Books by Darren Hibbs 115

Acknowledgements

I want to thank my family for allowing me the opportunity to write another book. I enter "the zone" when I write, and they are most gracious to allow me the space to do so.

To the Father, Son and Holy Spirit, I do not yet fully understand how the three of you work together, but I know that all of you together have given me these stories to encourage me and others. Thank you for the exhilaration that Your love, presence and voice provide.

I would never be able to write this or any book if it were not for my wonderful and gracious mother-in-law, Keri Wurbs. Thank you for your selfless care, tireless effort in prayer and your thoughtful and helpful editing.

Thank you to my editors for helping me make this book the very best it can be: Keri Wurbs, Christina Weeks and Judy Mwamba.

Lastly, I must thank my wife, Sarah. She has been on most of this journey with me, and what a wonderful trip it has been! I would never trade all of the ups and many downs for anything else just because I got to do them with you.

PREFACE

Many times, we do not receive from the Lord simply because we do not ask. A lot of those times it is because we do not even know we could or should ask. I have been given great license to ask anything from God because of the people I listened to and read who went before me. I pray that this book may serve the same for a new generation.

Ask the Lord to speak, act, heal, move and change your life, then don't stop asking until He does.

> *^{7}"Ask and it will be given to you; seek and you will find; knock and the door will be opened to you. ^{8}For everyone who asks receives; the one who seeks finds; and to the one who knocks, the door will be opened.*
>
> *Matthew 7:7-8*

> *^{1}Then Jesus told his disciples a parable to show them that they should always pray and not give up. ^{2}He said: "In a certain town there was a judge who neither feared God nor cared what people thought. ^{3}And there was a widow in that*

town who kept coming to him with the plea, 'Grant me justice against my adversary.'

⁴"For some time he refused. But finally he said to himself, 'Even though I don't fear God or care what people think, ⁵yet because this widow keeps bothering me, I will see that she gets justice, so that she won't eventually come and attack me!' "

⁶And the Lord said, "Listen to what the unjust judge says. ⁷And will not God bring about justice for his chosen ones, who cry out to him day and night? Will he keep putting them off? ⁸I tell you, he will see that they get justice, and quickly. However, when the Son of Man comes, will he find faith on the earth?"

Luke 18:1-8

A Diary of
DREAMS
AND
VISIONS

Chapter One

A DIARY

Ever since my childhood growing up in a strictly cessationist Baptist church, I have been fascinated by the supernatural gifts of the Holy Spirit in one way or another. I was taught explicitly and through subtle joking over many years that the gifts had ended with the closing of the canon of scripture. I was even taught that those who claimed to perform miracles, prophesy or speak in tongues today were either charlatans, lying, demonically possessed or deceived. So, I suppose my early fascination was with how irrelevant the gifts were to the Christian life today.

That is, in hindsight, a pretty radical position especially when viewed in light of scripture, but it was deeply held by a large portion of the American church while I was growing up.

Something happened to me that changed all that when I was fifteen. I began to question the cessationist teachings I was raised with when I started reading quite a bit of scripture and pondering whether it was really true. The answers I came to over the next several months caused to me question a lot of things.

~ Faithful To Scripture ~

I am happy to say that 99 percent of what I was taught growing up, I faithfully hold on to. My church was faithful to scripture to teach me the Word of God from a young age. I understood Jesus' atonement, God's love for me and His requirement of me to tell the world about Him. The one thing that fell suspect through a careful inspection of scripture was this one hang-up about spiritual gifts. I couldn't find anywhere in scripture that explicitly relegated miracles, tongues or prophecy to within the binding of my Bible. In fact, I found it taught exactly to the contrary.

But still, deeply held and ingrained teachings are hard to let go of. I carefully studied the reasons I had been taught that those things don't happen anymore, and I found some of the arguments very compelling but eventually without substance. One of the biggest reasons people chose not to believe in the continuation of the spiritual gifts was simply because they did not like many of the "charismatics" they had met. "They were a silly lot, unstable in all their ways," as it was thought, to the point of a complete distaste for everything they stood for.

Chapter One **A DIARY**

~ CONVINCED FROM SCRIPTURE ~

Mahatma Gandhi erred eternally in his thinking by saying, "I would be convinced to be a Christian were it not for the Christians I have met." We must not make the same mistake when it comes to our interpretation of scripture. We cannot "throw the baby out with the bath water."

So after many months, I was convinced from scripture that miracles, tongues and prophecy were for today and I set about seeking God earnestly for experiences in them. I prayed faithfully and unsuccessfully every day for years for God to speak through me or use me miraculously. Five years I prayed, actually, with no clear answer.

As with all change, it comes quickly at times and slow at others. My heart was slowly being changed in ways I could not see during those five years. And when change did come, it came quickly. Because after five years, God answered my prayers.

God actually began speaking to me in ways that were far beyond my expectations. The Lord spoke to me in dreams and through other people, and my life radically changed. Suddenly my belief in God wasn't just a deeply held position from scripture but truly the "assurance (evidence) of things I had hoped for but not yet seen" (Hebrews 11:1). It was as if I had experienced true faith for the first time. I knew without a shadow of a doubt now that God was real. And more importantly, I knew that He knew me and that He actually liked me!

~ Personal Stories ~

In this short book I will share many of my stories because I want to encourage you to pursue God for the same things I have discovered. I believe everything I have experienced is open game for all believers in Jesus, but I no longer feel the great need to argue my position. My reasons are simple:

1. I do not think cessationism is remotely defensible from scripture, and

2. I could not make my experiences happen; only God could. Therefore, since according to Hebrews 11:1 only God can give assurance (evidence), I feel no compulsion to try to convince others. Only God can do that for them.

I do not mean that to say that those who believe in cessationism are uneducated or not smart people. To the contrary, there are too many brilliant people to count who are cessationists. I am confident their belief comes from prejudice, not from study, something even the most brilliant human beings are susceptible to.

I have noticed something very interesting take place since the early 1990's in America: more and more people are relinquishing their cessationist beliefs in some form or fashion. Why? Because it is not tenable to believe against something you've experienced. The The Lord speaks and pours out supernatural experiences at a marvelous rate today!

~ CONVINCED FROM EXPERIENCE ~

I like to use the illustration of the lunar landing. There are still those around who persist that the whole thing was an elaborate hoax; that it never happened. No evidence to the contrary will sway them, because no evidence short of first-hand experience would be good enough for those conspiracy theorists. Even if the whole world were to believe their lies, there are a few people who could never be swayed: those with actual experience. You could never convince Neil Armstrong that he didn't set foot on the moon.

The same is true for believing that God still performs miracles and speaks today. You cannot convince someone otherwise when they have experience. Far too many people in the West have begun experiencing what our Christian brothers in the Eastern world have known for some time: God still acts among us in powerful ways.

There are fewer and fewer cessationist strongholds these days. Some still hold that God can move, but He just doesn't do it much these days. Some still cling to their beliefs and become more emboldened with every person who turns to the gifts of the Spirit. The move of the West to a more supernaturally-minded people has certainly reached a critical mass. I do not believe the majority of the church worldwide will ever again accept that God no longer operates miraculously today.

I have good reason to believe that. Like myself, more and more people are experiencing the supernatural goodness of God for themselves. Like Neil Armstrong, no arguments to the contrary could ever convince them otherwise. As a final thought, many cessationists hang up on that concept of experience. They believe our faith and practice should have nothing (or very little) to do with our own subjective experience–we must base everything upon the objectivity of scripture. Whereas that sounds perfectly noble, I have never met someone who actually walks that out.

~ Convinced by the Spirit ~

Experience is absolutely necessary for the Christian life. In fact, you cannot be born again unless you have had an experience with the Living God, His Son Jesus and the Holy Spirit. This is biblically clear from Peter, who told Jesus He was "The Christ, the Son of God." Jesus replied, "Blessed are you, Simon son of Jonah, for this was not revealed to you by man, but by my Father in heaven." (Matthew 16:17)

Even though Peter's answer could rationally and carefully be found throughout scripture, Jesus said it wasn't any teaching or self-study that led Peter to this conclusion. It was God himself. Peter's experience with the Living God informed his reality.

And that's our true reality. We cannot study scripture to know more about God, we must study scripture to experience more of God. It is only through experience that we can grow in God and lead others to Him.

In this book I'd like to share some of that experience with you. I pray you will be blessed by it.

Chapter Prayer

Lord, will You open my heart to hear from You through these stories?

Chapter Two
THE PEOPLE GOD LOVES

I was completely undone by what I was hearing. I couldn't believe such things existed. I had been asking and asking for five years with nothing to show for it, but then again, I wasn't totally sure what I had been asking for.

I was in the rugged mountains of Guatemala gazing listlessly out into the picturesque fields dotting the slope across the river. I was listening to a tape series about contemporary prophecy as I was sitting on my own bench in a retired American school bus the locals lovingly call a "chicken bus." The message shared the kinds of stories I had been asking for–the kinds of things that happened in the Bible–some of them even more amazing than what happened in the Bible, but maybe I thought that because they happened to someone today.

Chapter Two **THE PEOPLE GOD LOVES**

~ STORIES ENCOURAGE ~

I was listening to the most amazing stories I had ever heard in my life while looking out over the most beautiful mountainside I had ever seen when something stuck in my mind. I pulled off the headphones and looked as far across the mountaintops as I could. A thought kept running through my mind, and I couldn't shake it. I had not thought about it before, but now that it was there I couldn't get it out of my head.

I had given up my summer in college to travel to the most remote place on earth I had ever imagined. I could have stayed home and had fun at the beach like a lot of my friends, but I chose to raise money to travel to villages I had never heard of before to tell people about Jesus that I may never see again. Why? The words rang out over and over again in my head so loud I couldn't hear anything else.

"Because these are the people I love."

That phrase stuck with me powerfully during the remainder of my bus ride across western Guatemala. I smiled as I pondered the reality that God had sent me to tell some of the people He really loved about Himself. It made me happy that I got to be a part of touching God's heart.

~ THE PEOPLE ~

I melted back into gazing across the mountainside, this time without headphones in my ears. Our thirteen-hour trip was almost over, and I just wanted to soak up what the place looked like where the people God loves live. The hillsides were dotted with tiny little communities you could only spot because of a few puffs of smoke that rose from the trees. It felt like being sometime—not someplace—as if we'd stepped back into the distant past several hundred years ago.

We arrived at our destination, which happened to be the end of the road, literally. Our guide was happy to meet us all. Pablo was the same size as every other Guatemalan man I had met: 5'-3" tops, but his manner made him seem much taller than all the rest. He was jovial and engaging, and even with my abysmal lack of Spanish I instantly connected with him. He introduced us to what is known as the "Ixil Triangle" and went on to thank us for coming. Then he said something that still shocks me to this day.

"I want to thank you all for coming so far away from your homes. I know it was a big sacrifice for you all to be here, but I want to tell you why you all came here. You are all here because God loves these people. These are the people God loves. That is why you are here."

My jaw was gaping open, I'm sure. I understood enough of what he said in Spanish to know what he had said, but when our translator confirmed what I just heard, I was mesmerized. Mesmerized not by this small man who had just told me the meditations of my heart from 30 minutes earlier, but the fact that God was able to communicate to both of us the same phrase. The implications of this in real life were astounding!

~ GOD LOVES ~

It may seem small to you, but the fact that he used the very same sentence that resounded through my head before captured my attention. Maybe he had said that same thing to every mission team that came before me, but he didn't know what I was silently pondering a half hour before. What's more, I knew that I hadn't been actively thinking about it. My mind had been somewhere else when all of a sudden that phrase got planted in my brain, and I knew I hadn't put it there. At least, now I was sure I hadn't put it there.

I was in awe that I had clearly heard the voice of God as He proclaimed His love and intentions over these people. I thought I may have heard the voice of the Lord before, but I was never sure. This confirmed to me that I had heard the voice of God.

> *"My sheep hear My voice, and I know them, and they follow Me."*
>
> *John 10:27*

The joy I felt the rest of the day knowing that I had truly heard God's voice outweighed the gross neglect I had put into training my body for the rigors of mountain climbing we were currently engaged in. Every day seemed like we made at least six 4,000 vertical-foot ascents and descents. My body was exhausted beyond imagination, but my spirit was alive like I had never felt before.

~ Paying Attention ~

Since that time I have learned to pay attention to those little thoughts that run through my mind. I cannot recount to you the number of times this has happened since then, but you always remember that first time you know beyond a shadow of a doubt you heard God. I have also learned to pay close attention to people; especially when they are praying for me. I have found that when people pray for me they unknowingly pray the very sentences God put into my mind days or hours earlier. It is His way of letting us know that it was really Him.

I encourage you to start asking the Lord to speak to you every day. I asked every day for almost five years, and He did it. He did it profoundly that morning in the little village of Tsalbal, Guatemala.

But nothing prepared me for what I was going to experience next.

Chapter Two THE PEOPLE GOD LOVES

Chapter Prayer

Lord, will You show me the people around me that You love and speak to me about them?

Chapter Three

RAISING THE DEAD

We hiked into the village at dusk, and it was the first time in a week we didn't have a service scheduled. We were all so tired we went to bed fairly quickly. After going non-stop for what seemed like 24 hours a day, seven days in a row I slept like a rock, even with the giant next to me snoring loud enough to keep the rest of the village up. The next morning, I awoke to a sound I had never heard before, and one I will never forget.

A mother wailing is an unmistakable sound. It is a noise so distinct, you need not ask what happened to cause a woman to cry in such a way. It is a sound that transcends culture and language, and its memory still gives me chills twelve years later.

A woman in the village lost her three year-old son overnight and woke up to the grim discovery. Very quickly every friend in the village knew what hap-

Chapter Three RAISING THE DEAD

pened and was attending the family. All of us on our short-term mission team were at a loss for what to do. Very quickly, though, my teammates decided we should take up a collection to help pay for a funeral.

I was livid.

We were in Guatemala to share Jesus' love with the Ixil people. We were there to testify to all the things Jesus had done and what He had done for us in our lives. I don't remember Jesus ever paying for a funeral. In fact, I remember distinctly that He wrecked more than one by raising a person from the dead. We were not in Guatemala to pay for funerals. We were there to stop them!

My indignation quickly turned to boldness as I approached the long-term missionary and asked him if we could pray for the boy. Perhaps he thought I meant to ask if we could pray for the family–not the boy. He spoke with the family and they agreed to let us in the house. The wailing hadn't let up for a minute when I realized the missionary did not understand what I meant. I walked straight past the wailing mother and went over to the boy. The missionary stopped dead in his tracks at the door.

Undaunted, I approached the boy and kneeled down next to the bed he was laid out on. Covered by a burlap cloth, I never saw his face. The wailing stopped. The room was completely silent. I could see some of the team through the slats in the flimsy wooden wall, but I immediately focused on the boy. I was in a dilemma now, though.

Before we entered the room, I was filled with a confidence and boldness I had never experienced before in my life. I was not about to let a boy die while we were there when we could ask God to give him back. I knew God well enough to know that we should at least ask. Before I walked into the room I had a feeling He might just give me what I asked for. Then I walked into the room, and all my confidence vanished.

~ All Alone ~

I was left with myself and a dead boy. No confidence. No clue what I was doing. I felt all alone in that silent room—the loneliest I have ever felt in my life.

I couldn't retreat now. Alone or not, I still served a God who answers prayers and raises the dead. I laid my hand on the boy's chest and began to pray softly.

"God, give this boy back to his family. Raise this boy, please, I ask."

I went on like that for maybe five or ten minutes. I'm not exactly sure because it seemed like an eternity. I think it was just long enough for the missionary to get over his shock of what happened when we walked in and gather himself enough to come put his hand on my shoulder.

Chapter Three RAISING THE DEAD

"It's time to go," he whispered into my ear.

I hesitantly got up and followed him out past the teary-eyed mother and a host of family and friends. The boy was still dead, and I wanted more time. I obeyed the missionary, and we walked out. Looking back on it I wish I had told him to go on and I would stay. I wished I had stayed for another eight hours or longer—maybe God would have answered my prayers if I had stayed longer. In the moment I decided the missionary knew better about what would be culturally appropriate. My folly, only later did I realize, was that there is never a culturally appropriate way or time to raise a person from the dead. Never. Nowhere.

I came out of that house a broken spirit. I felt betrayed and let down by God. Where was He? Why did He leave me alone in that room? Why didn't He answer my prayer? As I begrudgingly pitched in for funeral expenses I wondered what would it have taken to raise that boy from the dead? Did I lack faith? Did I need more time? Was God willing?

Those questions haunted me for the remainder of my time in Guatemala. I felt like I didn't know what was up or down anymore. I was not sure if I had greatly failed God, or if God had greatly failed me. One thing was for sure, though; I became known as the guy who would pray for anything. Anything.

~ The Guy Who Prays ~

Every village we entered from that point on, there was always some dying cow or failing crop that needed prayer. I suppose the news that I was willing to ask God for anything spread through the remote mountaintops as I was the one praying for every person's smallest needs over the next two weeks.

By the time I returned to Texas my heart felt at an all-time low. I reckoned the trip to be a complete and utter failure. I reasoned that I was not missionary material because I couldn't handle the emotional turmoil of it.

My parents picked me up from the airport, and they were visibly disappointed by my utter sense of shock. I was in a fog, and they were expecting their same boy back. I wasn't the same boy, though. I never would be again. I was deeply wounded in a way I had never experienced before. I felt like God had completely forgotten and abandoned me when I needed Him the most.

As we drove along the highway from the airport my mother said something very curious to me. "Loretta wants to talk to you when you get home. She's got some things she wants to share."

Loretta was a fellow church member and friend of the family who had agreed to pray for me while I was gone.

"She said one night you were sweating and being attacked by little demons that looked like gnats, but I told her that was just silly because it was cold where you were because you were so high up in altitude," my mother continued. "I told her that wasn't possible."

"What did she say?" I quickly snapped back. I was instantly out of the fog. I was instantly awake.

"What did she say? She said I was sweating and being attacked by gnats?" I persisted.

"Well, yeah. Does that mean something?" Mom said, puzzled.

"I want to talk to her today," I said. "Not tomorrow. Today."

Mom didn't balk at my insistence. I wouldn't say another word about it, so she got Loretta over to the house that afternoon.

~ Demon Gnats ~

Loretta read from a prayer journal she kept. She told me the very day and hour she wrote down her experience. She had gone to sleep early that night and quickly awoke from a dream. She saw me sweating profusely, wrapped like a mummy and being attacked by little demons she could only describe as gnats. She said I was in agony and then I cried out to God to rescue me. That's when she woke up and prayed for me. She wrote it down that night and went back to bed.

I am rarely at a loss for words, but I couldn't eek out a syllable. My parents' concern over my strange state turned to an intense curiosity as they examined my dumbfounded face. I managed to collect my thoughts, and I told them the story.

Three weeks before we had hiked into a remote mountain village to show the Jesus film and share our testimonies. Unfortunately for everyone, the village was infested with gnats. I've never encountered a biting gnat before, but we were all being accosted by thousands of gnats that bit. It got really bad when we went to bed.

The rain started coming down hard. The eves of their houses are open, so the gnats took refuge in our shelter. I was in a twenty-degree "mummy" sleeping bag, and to keep the gnats off of me I would close it up and seal myself inside. My breath caused me to overheat and even though it was 50 degrees outside, I was sweating profusely. After several hours of sweating and then opening up long enough for a breath of fresh air that brought on a thousand more bites, I cried out to God.

"God, You've got to do something about this! I'm miserable."

Chapter Three **RAISING THE DEAD**

A minute later, our host came into our little room with the answer. A smoking corn cob in a coffee can. The thousands of gnats in our room left immediately. To me at that moment, it was one of the greatest miracles I had ever encountered. That may seem silly to be so happy to be free of biting gnats, but I was covered on every square inch of my body with welts from their bites. A month later I was still covered with the healing wounds of their miserable bites.

Loretta had no way of knowing what happened that night, but she showed me the time she woke up, and it was the exact time I had cried out to God. I remember because I thought I had made it through most of the night fighting off the gnats without sleep, and I was just ready to get up and leave the village. I decided to brave the gnats long enough to see my watch, and I realized it was only 11:30pm–the exact time Loretta had written down that she woke up from her dream.

~ THE GOD WHO SEES ~

I was amazed that she had seen me. She described the situation like she had been there. God showed another person, 1,500 miles away, countries apart, exactly what had happened to me. It turned out that five different times I had cried out for help on that trip, and five different times Loretta had a dream. Every single time she was able to tell me where I was, what the people I was with looked like and the exact words I said, because she had written her dreams down immediately.

That was the most amazing day of my life. I thought God had forgotten me. I thought I was alone. The whole time, God saw me and cared enough about me to show someone else. He wanted me to know that He cared about every moment of my life.

That day hearing Loretta tell me about what God had showed her changed my life. I am continually thankful that since then I have had many other times where God would speak directly and very personally to me.

Experiencing God speak directly to you changes you forever, and He wants all of us to experience that.

I encourage you to ask God to speak to you. Ask Him that every day for years until He does.

It is so worth it.

Chapter Prayer

God, will You speak to me and show me that You see me and care about me? Please give me the boldness to pray for things only You can do.

Chapter Four

GROWING IN THE PROPHETIC

<u>Growing in the Prophetic</u> is the title of a really good book by Mike Bickle, which I highly recommend. Much of what I know about prophecy I learned from he and Rick Joyner, Jack Deere and John Wimber. I am certainly in their debt for my early days of asking God to speak to me, because it was many of their stories that gave me the faith to ask.

And ask I did. For five years my adolescent heart asked God to speak. For five years I asked, and I don't remember a single answer until my mission trip to Guatemala. But after God spoke the first time, He didn't stop.

I don't want to start this out to make it sound like God speaks to me (or anyone else for that matter) on a consistent basis. If I were to quickly list every time

God has spoken to me here, it would sound like an unbroken chain of communication with God. That's just the nature of telling stories. When you tell them well, they always seem a little grander than they truly are.

The truth is that in a good year I have heard from the Lord five or more times. Since that Guatemala trip I have never heard from the Lord less than twice that I can remember. Even if God speaks ten times in a year, there are a lot of hours, days, weeks and months that God is not directly speaking, but I am always eternally grateful for when He does.

~ Ask And It Will Be Given ~

After I returned from Guatemala I received the shock of my life. Another human being had heard the very words I uttered only to God in prayer. God showed her in a dream the situation and the prayers I prayed. She prayed with me, and God answered both of us several times. That was a life-changing experience.

After you know that God can and will speak to you, it's like a drug you can never get enough of. I'm always hungry to hear God's voice more than I do now. I always want to ask God to speak more and more. I am constantly desiring to include God in every aspect of my daily life–even asking His opinion about the smallest detail.

God rarely seems to break in and speak for those small details, but the mystery of all mysteries is that sometimes He actually does! I don't understand why or when God will speak, but I do know that in my life there is a direct correlation between how much I ask and how often God speaks.

After Guatemala I settled back into college life. I was going to classes, leading Bible studies, chasing cute girls I hoped to be the future Mrs. Hibbs and having a great time with now life-long friends. I didn't stop asking God to speak, but I was happy that He had spoken to me once in five years. I would have been abundantly happy for once in five years, and I would still be grateful for that now. I never want to stop asking.

To my surprise, it wasn't too long before He answered again.

~ Passing Tests ~

I was taking a particular class that next semester that I was doing particularly well in. It was the first time I can remember actually enjoying my classes and my major in college. Early one morning I awoke in a dead sweat from a dream. It was on par with one of those standing-in-front-of-thousands-in-your-underwear dreams.

Chapter Four **GROWING IN THE PROPHETIC**

In the dream, I was in this particular class when the professor was handing back tests. When he got to my desk, he handed me mine, and to my horror it had a large, red "0" at the top.

I looked up at the professor and asked, "Why did you give me a zero?"

"Because you cheated," was his curt reply.

I became so immediately incensed in the dream that I started shouting profanities at him at the top of my lungs in front of the whole class. I am fairly certain I used words that I didn't know in real life. In the middle of my tirade the college dean walked in and told me he was kicking me out of school. I was immediately calm and now begging him to reconsider.

"No, you really blew it. You're gone," was his reply.

I stood there in the class horrified and embarrassed beyond imagination, and then I woke up.

~ PUTTING IT ALL TOGETHER ~

It took thirty minutes for the panic to wear off that morning, but when it finally did I went back to sleep. In college I had many dreams where I was being attacked by integrals or Charles Dickens, and I always rationed that they were from stress. This dream was different. The next morning after I woke up I could still remember it as clearly as if I were still in the dream. I thought about it some more and then blew it off as stress and went about my day. By 9:00 a.m. I had completely forgotten about it.

I forgot that later in the day I actually had to go to that class. I also didn't remember we had taken a test the week before. That afternoon when the class started I rushed in and sat down a minute late. In my hurry to get my notes out and get ready for class I hadn't noticed the professor was passing back our tests until he was standing over me. I had leaned down to put my backpack on the floor when I noticed him there holding a test out at me. I was speechless.

There was a big red "0" at the top with no other markings anywhere.

"Why did you give me a zero?" I asked.

"Because you cheated," was his curt reply as he started to walk off.

Moments like these are the ones where time stops. Before he had taken one step I am sure I had a month's worth of inner dialogue. The funny thing is that when I saw the zero I didn't remember the dream. When he said, "you cheated," I didn't remember the dream.

I know what you're thinking. "How could I possibly not remember the dream?" In the moment, it all happened so fast, and I had already written the dream off as stress. It just didn't occur to me.

That is, until what happened next.

In the moment where my professor said, "you cheated," and started to walk off, something strange happened inside of me. There are a lot of things that I can take, but being called a cheater or a liar is not one of them. In fact, every time I have been called a liar I get very angry. In this case I felt more anger and rage than I had ever experienced in my entire life, and it all came rushing on me in a nanosecond.

I was so enraged that this man would falsely accuse me of cheating and ruin my college career. The way the grading was structured, I could not have passed the class with a zero. If he really thought I had cheated, why did he give me a zero instead of turning me in? Cheating on a test in college is grounds for dismissal. Before I knew what was happening a rush of anger and filth came up inside of me, and the vilest words I could think of were just about to roll off my tongue to give him a piece of my mind. At the moment those words were on the tip of my tongue was when I remembered my dream.

I stopped dead in my tracks. Instead of shouting the words I wanted to at my professor, I sank back into my chair and quietly uttered, "Oh my God, what have you done?"

~ Does God Know What He's Doing? ~

When I awoke from my dream that morning one of the most shocking things about the dream was how I had lashed out at my professor. Don't get me wrong—I have a temper. As everyone who has ever truly known me can attest, my temper has never been aimed at people. For some silly reason I reserve my temper for inanimate objects that don't do as I please. Computers, cars, appliances and the like bear my wrath when they don't work, but I had never lashed out at a person before.

What I did in my dream was inconceivable to me. I was sure that I wasn't capable of that. Right up until the moment it happened.

That's the way it is with sin. All sin is bad, but the truly dangerous ones are those we think we are not susceptible to; the ones we think we have conquered once and for all.

> *All kinds of animals, birds, reptiles and creatures of the sea are being tamed and have been tamed by man, but no man can tame the tongue. It is a restless evil, full of deadly poison.*
>
> *James 3:7-8*

James makes it clear that no one has enough control over their tongue not to sin, but I thought I had achieved some higher level of purity than he understood. God used the most bizarre exclamation point that day to make sure I understood my place.

I didn't hear a single word my professor said that day during class. I was completely inside my own head the whole time. There was a whole swirl of thoughts and emotions. I couldn't believe that not only was I capable of that kind of defiling speech, I would absolutely have done it had not God warned me. Then I couldn't believe that God had warned me. He cared enough about me to reach down and steady my hand from very destructive sin. Then I was tormented because I knew I couldn't pass the class (which I had to for graduation) with a zero. God hadn't shown me any resolution in my dream, only what would have gone wrong. What was I supposed to do?

I was in serious trouble, but I had an amazing amount of peace. This was the second occasion God had, beyond a shadow of a doubt, spoken to me. I always thought dreams were supposed to be dark mysteries and riddles. I didn't know what to do with one that actually happened in real life exactly as it was in the dream (except that I didn't blow up). I thought about Joseph's dream to leave Bethlehem with Jesus and Mary (Matthew 2:13-15), and I realized that our loving God will sometimes warn us before destruction (at our hands or someone else's). God is amazingly good that way.

But I was still in trouble and I didn't know what to do. I just knew I had to do something if I didn't want to fail.

~ High Marks ~

After the class I went up to my professor and very respectfully asked him to reconsider. I assured him that I hadn't cheated, and he very confidently and angrily assured me that he wasn't going to reconsider. I left the class very perplexed.

Why would God warn me only to have me fail the class? I couldn't understand it, but I knew that the same good God who warned me could fix the situation. I had no idea how that would happen, but I was confident He could do it. I just knew that my part was to rise above the darkness that I was just now aware of hiding in my heart.

I did not know what to do. I had no plan. I only knew that I had to trust that God would help me. I had made up my mind, though, that even if I failed the class I was going to make sure I never resorted to my flesh that was clamoring for justice and vindication.

Still confused, I went to the next class a couple days later. My professor started out the class giving me something to worry about. He came by my desk before class started and told me he wanted to speak with me after class. I couldn't lose the lump in my throat

Chapter Four **GROWING IN THE PROPHETIC**

the whole class. I was sure he was going to tell me he was turning me into the dean and I would be expelled. Again, I don't remember a word my professor said that day. I had enough going on inside my head.

I fearfully went forward after everyone had left the class and said, "You wanted to see me?"

"Darren, I know you can't pass the class with a zero. I still think you cheated, but I can't prove it. I'll give you a fifty on the test."

A fifty wasn't great, but I knew that I could pass the class with it. I'd take it! I hastily handed him my test and he marked out the big red "0" and put a big red "50" next to it.

As he handed it back to me I said, "I know I can't prove it either, but I promise I didn't cheat. But thank you for this. Thank you very much."

I walked out with a little bounce in my step. God had made a way for me to pass the class! I was so excited. God really had come through for me.

The next week I happened to be walking through the professors' office building needing to talk to a different professor about a class assignment. As I walked past my "you cheated" professor's office door, he spotted me and called my name. I didn't even know where his office was up to that point. I quickly poked my head inside his door.

"Yes sir?"

"Darren, I've been thinking about it a lot, and I don't think you cheated. Do you have your test with you?"

I was at a complete loss for words. I quickly realized that just by chance the test had never left my backpack, so I pulled it out and handed it to him. He took his big red pen and scratched out the "50" and put a "100" next to it. The test now had at the top a zero and a fifty marked through and a perfect grade in their place. There were no other marks on the test. I knew he never even bothered to grade it.

"Thank you, thank you, thank you!" I gushed as I shook his hand and bounced out of his office.

If I had a bounce in my step for a fifty, you can imagine my excitement over the hundred. I was so excited that I completely forgot about the meeting with the other professor I was in the building to see. I ran back to my apartment and worshipped God for His goodness, provision and His love. I'd never felt so overwhelmed by God's hand in my life before then.

The message was clear. "Darren, you were going to fail this test if I hadn't warned you, but you passed the test with a 100!" I still kick myself to this day that I lost that test. I wish I had it around as a memento. I should have framed it! Still, I couldn't have been happier and that was the conclusion of that matter.

Or so I thought.

~ THE END FROM THE BEGINNING ~

God is really smart. I mean REALLY smart. He knows a lot more about what's going on than we do. In fact, He knows it all. Not only is He really smart; He is really good at orchestrating some pretty cool stuff that we couldn't imagine in our wildest dreams.

My wife, Sarah, had a friend in high school. Her father was a professor at the university, so she had grown up in town with a lot of other professor's kids. One of them was a young man from another country, and he didn't have a lot of friends in high school because of that. He had friends, but that feeling of loneliness that every adolescent experiences at times was only heightened by the cultural differences he faced. But my wife's beautiful heart reached out to him. She would invite him to sit with her and her friends occasionally or invite him to partake in outings with them.

They seemed like small gestures to her, but they meant the world to him during those formidable years. During college the two didn't stay in close contact, but they would keep up from time to time. After he found out Sarah and I were engaged, he wanted to invite us over to his parents' house to experience some of their ethnic cultural food. I love getting to meet and eat with people of other cultures, because I love the diversity that God has created. I love to experience it. We happily agreed and were off to eat with him and his parents a few days later.

We were greeted by Sarah's friend at the door, and when we walked into the house and met his parents in their kitchen, time stopped again.

The faded memories of that dream and test from several years earlier came rushing back in an instant. I couldn't believe what was happening. Sarah's friend was the son of my professor. They weren't believers, and I instantly knew that there was a lot more going on with God's warning than me passing that class.

They were Muslims who God greatly desired to follow Him. If I had blown it all those years earlier, they may have never had an opportunity to follow Jesus. The very sight of me might have turned them away from God forever if I had not heeded my dream, but thank God I did!

After everything that happened I thought about Joseph. He had a very clear dream that his father and brothers would bow down to him as their ruler. Amazingly, that actually happened, but it was a long, hard journey for Joseph getting there. But Joseph was patient.

We are so often wrapped up in the temporal affairs of our lives. When we ask God to speak, He often has plans that go far beyond the simple request we have for this week. We just have to be faithful to walk out the journey fully trusting God.

Chapter Four GROWING IN THE PROPHETIC

No one does it perfectly, but for everyone it starts with asking. Will you ask God to speak to you? Will you be faithful to listen? Will you be trusting of God when it takes patience to see the fulfillment?

By God's grace, I know the answer can be "yes."

Chapter Prayer

Lord, please speak to me and show me the things on Your heart for me today. I long to hear Your voice.

Chapter Five

A BROTHER'S DREAM

Japan is a beautiful place. The people, the hospitality and the culture is something I can easily say was one of the best experiences of my life. I know that was greatly aided by the number of wonderful Japanese Christians so willing to take my team and I in and show us their marvelous country. It was truly a great time for me.

I had been praying a lot before this mission trip. I had a year under my belt now since my Guatemala trip, and the Lord had already spoken a few times through dreams to me, so I was excited about going to Japan to share the gospel with one of the most unreached nations on earth. After the ways the Lord had spoken and moved in my life in the past year, I was sure He was going to have much to say about this trip.

I knew God cared about His people who were yet to follow Him. I knew He cared about me. I was sure

Chapter Five A BROTHER'S DREAM

God was going to speak in dramatic ways to increase our ministry in Japan. I prayed and fasted and asked God to show up. I knew He would.

For months leading up to my team's trip to Japan we had problems. I had to convince two different team members not to drop out. They were afraid they weren't going to be able to go for various reasons. I assured them God always comes through and to hang in there. I had to whisper a prayer under my breath each time I reassured them asking God to "please come through." Come through He did. Just in time God provided everything we needed to be on our way for a successful trip. Even though I'd not heard anything prophetic from Him before the trip I felt like I'd seen Him move powerfully just to get us there.

I was excited to be in Japan once we landed. It was instant culture immersion, and I loved it. I was just waiting for God to start speaking to me about which Japanese person I met was going to come to know Him. I was waiting for God to reveal to me the secrets of the hearts of those around me so that what Paul said would happen:

> *But if an unbeliever or someone who does not understand comes in while everybody is prophesying, he will be convinced by all that he is a sinner and will be judged by all, and the secrets of his heart will be laid bare. So he will*

> *fall down and worship God, exclaiming, "God is really among you!"*
>
> *1 Corinthians 14:24-25*

The ministry we were engaging in was exciting, but I kept waiting. I kept waiting and asking. I asked the Lord to speak a lot, but no matter how much I asked I got nothing from the Lord. I didn't hear from God about a single person in Japan, but our ministry went really well. We actually had a tremendous impact on the little church we ministered at, and they had an even bigger impact on us. They were so good to us, and I have such a special love for them even today.

~ Confidence Waning ~

After about four weeks in country I wondered if God was going to speak. I had figured, incorrectly, that God was surely going to speak clearly when I went on a mission trip. I knew He would have lots to say to start a revival in Japan. I do know He wants to start a revival in Japan, but it obviously wasn't through prophetic evangelism while I was there.

One evening I was crying out to God before I fell asleep. I begged Him to speak. I asked Him if He really cared about these people like He cared about the Guatemalans. Then I instantly retracted that. I knew He did, but I told Him I didn't understand why He spoke to me about seemingly trivial things over the past year. Now, when I was doing the Lord's highest

Chapter Five A BROTHER'S DREAM

calling in Japan (what I thought then), He had nothing to say, and it wasn't for lack of me paying attention.

I fell asleep that night wondering why God was so quiet now. Had I done something? Was it me? My confidence in the God who spoke was definitely shaken.

About 4 am I awoke from a dream sobbing. I had never experienced anything like it. I was actually sobbing uncontrollably when I woke up, and I couldn't stop for thirty minutes. It was out of my control, and it was beyond my understanding.

The dream was short. I saw my older brother in prison. He was in a big "tank" as they often call them. I've been involved in prison ministry before, so I know a little about prison life. A tank is like a big dorm where everyone's bunk is in a giant open room. They may have thirty or more men all in the same room, so they make more efficient use of their space. The people in the tanks are usually the more docile guys; they reserve the small cells for the ones they can't trust.

In the dream my brother sat on his bed in the big, open room. Just then a group of thugs came up to him and surrounded him in a circle. They mocked him and made some comments about how his mouth had gotten him in trouble. I watched the whole thing as if I was twenty feet up and twenty feet away. I had a bird's eye view of the whole thing.

Immediately I was overcome with emotion. I knew they were going to kill my brother. I wanted to shout out, "NO!" but I was mute. I felt helpless. I knew my brother was. He had palsy in one of his arms, so I knew he didn't have a chance at defending himself against the angry mob.

One of them took out a shiv, a makeshift knife, and advanced at my brother with it. He desperately tried to talk his way out of the situation, but there was no use. As the man drew closer to my brother he swiped horizontally at him as if to slit his throat. My brother dodged, but in the process the bridge of his nose was slit. I could see the blood gushing from his nose from a horizontal slice right where the bone meets the cartilage.

Just as I saw all this I was finally able to shout, "NO!" The only problem was I realized I was awake now. My shout was probably heard throughout the neighborhood, and I was out of control. I couldn't stop my sobbing. For the only night my entire stay in Japan I was sleeping in my own room, so my roommate never saw it. For thirty minutes I couldn't stop crying. I sobbed and cried out to God to save my brother. He had to come through for him. I begged God to rescue him. I pleaded for angels to be released to his aid.

Chapter Five **A Brother's Dream**

The dream felt so real that I couldn't distinguish dream from reality. After the sobbing stopped I still had a burden for prayer for another half hour. For an entire hour after my dream I cried out for my brother in prayer. Pleading and begging I longed for the dream to be just that. Then finally, after an hour, the feeling of dread and helplessness left. The burden for prayer left.

I was so tired I fell right back asleep.

~ Confusion ~

The next morning when I woke up, quite drowsy from losing an hour of sleep, I couldn't make sense of my dream. I wondered if it was an allegory the Lord had given me about the Japanese people in response to my pleas for Him to speak. I was confused because if it was God speaking to me about the Japanese people I was no better off than the day before. If it was God speaking, I'd need another dream or prophet just to figure out what the dream meant.

A couple days later after wrestling with the dream's meaning I decided to email my mother. I thought there was a chance the dream was actually about my brother. I know that seems obvious now, but in the midst of all my crying out to God to speak about the Japanese I was sure He'd answered, and I just wasn't getting it.

I asked my mother if my brother was doing well. I said I had a dream about him, and he was in trouble. I wasn't going to tell my mother he was attacked. You just don't ever tell a mother something like that.

What happened next really surprised me. My mother was overly interested in knowing what my dream was. Then she told me that my brother had been attacked in prison. I hadn't told her that; only that he was in trouble.

When I had come back from my trip to Guatemala the year before, my parents were in the room when our friend Loretta was telling me the dreams she had and how they were exactly what was going on while I was there. It was a new experience for all of us, and I think it had left an impression on my parents the same as me. God speaking in dreams and things like that was new to all of us, but I think my mother had really taken to heart the fact that God could and would still speak like that. When it came to one of her sons, she was going to take it seriously.

The rest of my time in Japan flew by. We had a great time finishing up the ministry we were involved in over the next two weeks. I still love Japan and I long to go back. I have not had the opportunity in over a decade, but my heart longs for Japan more than any place on earth. They are a beautiful people who have a great need for the gospel.

Chapter Five A BROTHER'S DREAM

~ MEETING UP ~

When I got back from Japan I had one thing in mind. I had to go to prison and visit my brother. I had to find out if what I had dreamed was real. After a couple days of jet lag and catching up with my parents and friends I made the four-hour drive to visit him. I wasn't prepared for what I was going to see. If someone had described it to me, I don't think I would have believed it. If someone had sent a photo I would have been skeptical that it was a fluke or Photoshopped.

As I sat across the table from my brother I was speechless. He had a healing scab across his nose right at the bridge where cartilage meets bone. The cut that was healing wasn't sort of in the same place I'd seen in the dream but in the exact place. It looked one hundred percent like what I had seen—a clean cut straight across his nose.

As we sat there and talked about it, and later with my mother, I realized that my dream had been within an hour of when he was attacked in real life. I was asleep, dreaming on the other side of the planet, and my brother was being attacked back here during the day. God surely knows no time zones.

I'm convinced that God showed me my brother's peril now because He always longs to include and partner with His people in every way. God hears our prayers, and He longs for us to join in with His purposes and plans. I know God has great plans for my brother, and

He wanted me to know the trouble he was in so I could intercede for him. God wanted my partnership in the situation the same way He'd used Loretta a year before. I was in trouble and crying out to God, and He showed a woman through dreams and visions. My brother was in trouble, and He showed me.

God really cares about us!

~ Questions We Don't Ask ~

I learned something important through that experience. I still ask God to speak about specific situations, like my ministry in Japan, but I no longer expect Him to answer the exact question I ask. Think about the number of times Jesus refused to answer people on earth with a straight answer. He often posed another question to them entirely, or His answer almost seemed to have nothing to do with the question. There are too many examples of this to list here.

Why did Jesus answer questions this way? Because He is a lot smarter than we are. Often our questions are based in preconceived notions that we're correct about something. Jesus knows our hearts so well that instead of answering our questions directly, He'll often go back to the root issue that created our question in the first place and deal with that. Sometimes we're so removed from the root issue that the answer (or question as it often is) seems nonsensical to us. It certainly did to the Pharisees over and over again.

Chapter Five **A BROTHER'S DREAM**

What I learned was that when I ask for God to speak, I have to be open to hearing what He wants to talk about. He sees everything that is going on, and I need to trust Him that if He speaks, whatever He says is for sure the most relevant thing for me to know at that moment. I'm no longer disappointed when God doesn't answer my question directly. It doesn't stop me from continuing to ask questions because God still answers those even when He's dealing with us on separate issues, but I always take whatever He says with a great deal of seriousness.

I encourage you to write your dreams down. Journal your prayers and questions from God, and definitely begin to ask Him to speak to you. He loves to speak to people who are asking and listening intently.

Chapter Prayer

Lord, give me grace to remember to write down what You speak to me. Give me an ear to hear what Your Spirit is saying.

Chapter Six

SEPTEMBER 11, 2001

I was still in college at the time, so like any good college student I woke up at 9:00 a.m. I had taken a semester off from classes for a mandatory internship with a company in town, but I didn't start for another week so I was killing time that week.

All my roommates had early classes, so I was the only one in the apartment at the time. We didn't watch television much so our little 13-incher sat unused most of the time. I was happily enjoying breakfast when my sister called.

"Hey, Stephanie. Aren't you supposed to be in class?"

"Darren," she said with a shaky voice, "the World Trade Center just collapsed. They ran planes into it."

That's just morbid, I thought. You don't joke about this kind of thing. I really thought she was pulling my leg.

Chapter Six SEPTEMBER 11, 2001

"Sure they did, sis. Sure they did," I calmly replied. I was sure she was joking and there was some bigger prank tied into it. That's just how we rolled.

"No, really. Turn on the TV."

I turned on our little white television, and the tube buzzed to life. It was very old so the picture took almost a full minute to come to life, but the audio came on instantly. The tone in the newswoman's voice instantly sent shivers down my spine.

When the picture came on the first thing I saw was the video loop we've all seen a thousand times since then. I watched as Tower 2 collapsed, and I fell to my knees. I'm not sure if I ever hung up the phone or said goodbye.

I watched in horror as those two buildings collapsed. I was angry at myself for waking up so late. The world was crumbling around me, and I hadn't even been awake for when they fell.

All I could think was, "why hadn't I done something about it?"

~ AUGUST 25TH ~

When I returned from my mission trip to Japan, I was ready to turn the world upside down. I had just arrived back in College Station, and my friends and I were going to the international student housing witnessing to the newcomers from all over the globe.

It was a great time, and I was enjoying some of the best prayer times in my life. I had never enjoyed my walk with Jesus more. Saturday evening, August 25th I'd been praying about our college church group before going to bed. I really wanted God to speak to me about our service the next morning. I asked God to show me what He was thinking about for them.

When I finished my prayer time I went and laid down in my bed. I said a quick prayer that I'll never forget just before my head hit the pillow.

"God, I'm Yours. Speak to me as You will."

When I laid down and closed my eyes, immediately I saw a vision. I'd never experienced anything like this before. I was still fully awake, but I was seeing something on the back of my eyelids as if it were a movie in front of me. I'd always heard people talk about visions and sometimes I wondered if it was just their imagination. This was not my imagination.

I saw someone wrapped up like a mummy, desperately trying to get out of their bandages. I couldn't hear anything, but the person was wrapped so tightly I could see the expression on their face. The person was in great agony, and he was on fire. The fire was causing the person to writhe about and scream, but I heard no noise. I could see through the bandages a mouth open

Chapter Six **SEPTEMBER 11, 2001**

and close as if to shout "Help! Help me!" Then the vision ended.

I was so disturbed by what I saw that I sat up in bed and opened my eyes. I thought to myself, "what was that?" I pondered what it meant. Could God be telling me that someone at the college student church service tomorrow felt like they were wrapped up, burning and dying? Was someone silently crying out for help?

I laid back down and went to sleep. The next morning I pondered what it meant and went to church. I told our college pastor that I thought someone there might feel like they were trapped and burning and crying out for help. In the end I thought even if I had interpreted the vision wrong, that's always a safe bet for emotional college students. A few people responded and went forward for prayer at the end.

I was still perplexed by what I saw. I had taken a stab at interpreting the vision, but I wasn't sure I was right. The vision had been so gruesome I am still disturbed to this day when I think about it.

~ SEPTEMBER 1 ~

A week had passed, and I was a little discouraged. I was ready to start my internship, but the company had some "big things" come up and they pushed my start date back. Instead of being at work for a week now, it was going to be another two before I started. I was afraid they were going to back out on me, and I was going to have blown a semester off of college and still have to get another internship.

I prayed that evening and asked God to break in for me. I needed the company to let me start, because as it was I would barely have enough weeks at work for my internship to count. I told the Lord I trusted Him because He had never let me down before.

As I climbed into bed I thought about the previous Saturday evening. I remembered my prayer, and I thought I would try it again. Maybe the Lord would speak to me again about something through another vision.

I'm not right very often, but when I am sometimes I think it is worse than being wrong. I prayed my little prayer and put my head on my pillow and closed my eyes. Just like the Saturday night before I instantly had a vision.

This time I saw people's faces passing in front of me from right to left. They weren't mummified, but there was fire in the background just like the week before. As each new face passed in front of me they would get closer for a moment and scream out in agony, then they would shrink back as they passed out of sight. Each new face was a new tortured soul crying out in pain for help. Their pain was so great that when they shouted their jaws looked like the unhinged mouths of feeding snakes.

Chapter Six SEPTEMBER 11, 2001

I hadn't thought it would be possible, but this vision was far more disturbing than the week before. When the vision ended I had seen probably twenty to thirty faces crying out to me. They were burning and in agony. I couldn't figure out how that had anything to do with our college ministry, but I figured God had spoken to me about them since I asked.

The next morning I again reported to my college pastor that I felt like there might be people who whose "world is on fire" and they need help. Both Sundays he relayed that and there was a good response during the prayer time, so I thought I'd done well. I thought it was God's answer to my prayers.

~ THE WHOLE STORY ~

At the time I didn't know any better. Now I know when I have a dream or vision, it's always important to not just relay what I think may be the interpretation, but also to tell exactly what I saw.

Even after the several dreams I'd had that turned out to be literal, I still thought that most of what God gives us is supposed to be vaguely figurative and hard to understand. A lot of times it is, but we never fully know so it's always better to tell the WHOLE story.

I don't know what would have changed if I had told my college pastor what I had seen. Maybe nothing. Maybe God would have shown to everyone how much

He loves us and likes to share what's on His mind with us. I'll never know.

~ SEPTEMBER 9 ~

The evening of September 8th, I went to bed knowing what was going to happen. Two Saturday nights in a row I had visions just after my head hit the pillow. I had the formula. I knew what would happen tonight.

I said my prayer, and I put my head on the pillow and closed my eyes.

Nothing.

I waited for a moment and then I sat back up and opened my eyes.

"That didn't work," I thought to myself. "I'll try it again. Maybe I just need another go at it. Lord, I'm Yours. Speak to me as You will."

I know now that's silly and at the time I felt a little silly doing it, but I figured it couldn't hurt. I laid my head back on the pillow and closed my eyes again. Again, I saw nothing.

"Well, it happened twice and that's all," I mused. "That's okay. I know You love me, Lord. I love You too," I prayed.

I drifted off to sleep convinced the Lord had chosen not to speak to me that night. Just then I opened my

Chapter Six **SEPTEMBER 11, 2001**

eyes, and I was in Manhattan. At least, I thought I was. I've never been there, but from all the pictures I had seen it looked just like it. The dream was so real I didn't know it was a dream. This was one of the most vivid and real dreams I have ever had. It's also the only dream I ever had with an angel.

I walked along the streets of Lower Manhattan with a guide. He was a man about six feet tall wearing a white robe. I knew then he was an angel and that didn't seem surprising to me in the dream. In fact, I felt very comfortable with him.

~ A City So Nice They Named It Twice ~

I'm a construction guy, and I've always wanted to visit New York. I don't know why I never have, but it's just never happened. I've been to LA, Tokyo, London, Istanbul and many other large cities, but never New York–the city I've always been most fascinated by. I'd always wanted to stroll the streets and look up at the buildings that would dwarf me.

But most of all, I had wanted to go to the observation deck of the World Trade Center. I wanted to know what it felt like to stand atop New York and gaze out across the vast sea of concrete and contemplate how cool it was that God let man realize such a dream like New York.

All this was a running monologue with my angel guide. I was following him and my mouth was just running. I was the chattiest I'd ever been in my whole life. I was telling him of all the places I'd longed to visit in New York. He never said a word which left the door open for me to talk all the more. I kept telling him how excited I was to finally be in New York. There were so many places I'd longed to see.

The angel was intense, though. He never spoke. He seemed completely gripped by something. He was leading me along as we walked side by side, but he wasn't interested in my conversation. A couple of times I'm sure I saw him glance over at me and roll his eyes. It didn't bother me, though, and I kept talking.

Then he abruptly stopped. He turned and gazed at the twin towers of the World Trade Center. When he stopped I finally shut up. I looked at his eyes and saw pain. He held out his hand with an open palm as if to point at the towers. I followed the end of his extended hand out to see the towers.

He was so intense I didn't say another word, I just stood there and watched. I didn't know what he wanted me to see. Everything looked normal, just as I'd seen it in photos.

Just then, both towers collapsed. They descended straight down into the ground. I was shocked and perplexed because I thought a tall building like that

Chapter Six **SEPTEMBER 11, 2001**

would fall over if it collapsed, but they both went straight down.

My eyes felt like they were bulging out of my head. Suddenly there were thousands of terrified people streaming towards us. They raced past us as we both stood silently still. Their faces were unforgettable. I've never seen such terror before.

For some reason I was unmoved by the situation. I couldn't feel what was going on. I was emotionless except for the feeling of being cheated. With thousands running past us in shock and terror I turned to my angel guide and said the dumbest thing to ever come out of my mouth.

"Well, that sucks! Now I'll never get to go up into the observation deck!"

I look back on it now and I think the poor angel felt like he drew the short straw with me. He was completely gripped by the situation except when I said that. He seemed to hang his head in exasperation. When I saw that, I instantly realized the gravity of the situation. Suddenly, I was aware of what was happening.

This was serious. My attitude changed and now I could see clearly. The World Trade Center had just collapsed, and the city was completely in shock.

~ Rebuilding ~

Now that I got it the angel seemed a little less put out with me. He lowered his hand by his side but never stopped looking away from the site. The people weren't rushing by anymore. Then he raised his hand again. I looked back and in the place of the World Trade Center a small white building was built in it's place.

I saw it built in about five seconds and on top they placed an amphitheater. The building was only about five stories tall and people gathered on the roof and a worship concert broke out. I could hear the people singing worship songs to God for His provision.

I felt hope that in the place of devastation there was worship and thankfulness to God, but I was disappointed that the building was so small. I felt let down that it seemed so few people showed up to thank God for His goodness. The dream ended on that note, and I awoke already in prayer asking God to raise up worship for Himself in New York.

~ Making Sense of It All ~

When I realized I was awake, I began to ponder the dream. It was so real, so vivid that it was hard to separate reality from dream. I knew it was a dream, but I couldn't figure out what it meant beyond being for our college group again. I had awakened early on the

Chapter Six **SEPTEMBER 11, 2001**

---

morning of Sunday, September 9th, and I figured God must be speaking to me again about our group.

The next morning I told our college pastor that I thought maybe there were people in the room who "felt like their world was falling down." I so wish now I'd told someone what I'd seen. I feel so stupid not telling anyone the actual dream. It's a mistake that I don't think has happened since.

I didn't think anything of the dream again until I heard the words on the news that morning. Before the picture on our old tube television ever came on I remembered my dream. Then when I saw what happened that terrible day in New York I'm pretty sure I dropped the phone. It was surreal. I think I heard my sister's faint voice in the background.

I sat there glued to the television for the next six hours it seemed. Over and over again I couldn't let go of the thought that was going through my head.

Why hadn't I said anything? Why hadn't I called someone? Why did God show me that and then allow me to do nothing?

I felt horrible. I thought I had let God down. He showed me something so I could save thousands of lives and I'd failed. That evening I drove my car to the emptiest parking lot in town, and I just cried. I cried for hours. So many people died, and I did nothing. I said nothing. I felt like I had blood on my hands.

~ What Do We Do With Dreams? ~

It took me months to get over that feeling of devastation. It took years for me to realize that if I had called anyone, I'd probably be sitting in Guantanamo right now. Months later I realized there wasn't anything I could have done. Nobody in New York was going to listen to some college student in Texas about a premonition he had about the most iconic buildings in the city.

Furthermore, I didn't even know when that was going to happen. I could have called Mayor Giuliani and evacuated the towers but I had no clue when it would happen. God didn't tell me the dream was literal, and He didn't tell me it was going to happen two days later. It could have happened ten years later for all I knew.

Every evening when I came home from work (which finally started) I pondered all this. I had to put it out of my mind during work, or it consumed me and the emotions overcame me. I think I cried every evening for months. I was just too sure I had failed God.

When I finally had the epiphany that nothing I could have done would have changed anything, I wondered why God would have shown me all that. Why would God tell me something I wasn't supposed to act on?

Chapter Six **SEPTEMBER 11, 2001**

I've since come to understand that not everything God does has to make sense at the time. Sometimes God tells us things because He calls us friends.

I no longer call you servants, because a servant does not know his master's business. Instead, I have called you friends, for everything that I learned from my Father I have made known to you. (John 15:15)

Sometimes God just wants to share what's on His heart with a friend. Other times there's a long leadtime to understand what's really going on.

~ Finding Peace ~

It took a while, but I finally felt peace about that day. God knew what was going to happen, and He was grieved about it. The angel was so intense, I believe, because he knew the events weren't going to be stopped. People were going to die, and God's heart was moved over it.

My visions had been a precursor to my dream. I had seen the misery that caused people to choose to leap to their death headfirst from those buildings instead of burning to death. What a terrible moment and it was all on God's heart.

I'm not going to debate whether it was God or Satan that caused 9/11 because frankly I'm still not sure. In fact, I don't really care to know. What I do know is that the heart of a compassionate God was moved with sadness over the events of that day. I'm sure God knew then what we know now: that the events of September 11, 2001 would unleash on earth a new level of war, pain and destruction that hasn't ended to this day.

I believe that most of the dream is obviously literal. I can't tell you how close the actual events resembled what I saw in my dream. But the little building that grew up in place of the towers never happened. I think this was a figurative part of the dream. Whereas New York has in almost every way grown further away from God in the past decade, I think for a short time there was quite a revival in the Big Apple. Immediately after the tragedy there was a sense of awe and wonder of God. Many put their faith in Him in the days following, but compared to the overall size of the city I think it was small and short-lived. But small and short as it was, it was very important to God. There are numerous accounts of God moving people to New York at just the right time, and they reaped a harvest.

Even though I felt peace about my dream I still questioned God almost daily as to why He showed me. I got my answer a little over a year later.

It wasn't until 2011 that it all made sense, but I tell that story in more detail in my book, <u>The Year of the Lord's Favor?,</u> available at Amazon.com. (A sample chapter is included at the end of this book)

Chapter Six SEPTEMBER 11, 2001

Chapter Prayer

Lord, show me how I can be a part of bringing change and righteousness back to my nation. Lord, speak to me about what You think about my city, state and nation today.

Chapter Seven

PROPHETS

I was seven days into a 21-day fast. I felt miserable, weak and silly for doing it. I didn't know what I was thinking anymore. I wanted to eat so badly my right arm looked appetizing, and I couldn't see any reason why I shouldn't. Eat food that is, not my right arm.

I had been confident that it was God who had called me to fast for 21 days, but by day seven I was sure I'd made it up myself. There are lots of people out there that will tell you all the health benefits of fasting, but I don't care. If God's not watching me I'm not doing it. If He doesn't care if I fast or eat, I'm eating, no bones about it. I don't fast for health reasons; I fast so I can feel God.

I decided to make a deal with God. I knew by now He could speak. Most of the time when I asked Him a specific question that had a time-frame I didn't get an answer, but I still knew God could speak to me about it if He wanted to so I thought I'd give Him the opportunity. I told the Lord that if this really was Him calling me to fast for 21 days I needed to hear it from Him. I didn't know any prophets personally, but I did know He spoke to prophets a lot more often that He did to me. I told God I could really use one right then. My deal was that I was going to eat at 7:00 pm that evening if I hadn't heard from Him. I specifically asked God for a prophet to tell me I should be fasting.

Don't take that the wrong way. I wasn't testing or challenging God. I'd already decided to eat; I was just giving God an opportunity to speak and correct me if I was wrong. That's always a good thing to do. God has spoken numerous times since then to correct me, and I'm always thankful I have a Father who loves to keep me out of trouble.

I drove home from work that evening waiting for God to call me on the telephone, but it never came.

~ Time's Up ~

7:00 p.m. came and went, so I decided to break my fast early with the best thing I could think of at the time: popcorn. For whatever reason I had a serious craving for buttery, greasy popcorn after having not eaten for seven days. God hadn't spoken to me so I pulled open the hot, steamy bag and dug in. I think I might have burned my mouth on the first bite.

About a third of the way through the bag I got a call. I had spoken twice with this guy named Draper up to this point, so I was curious why he was calling me at this very moment. Draper seemed to fancy himself a person who heard from God, but I was skeptical. He had called me before with two very flattering "words from God," but I don't do flattery.

Still, I was excited and afraid all at the same time. What if Draper was actually going to tell me that God wanted me to fast? What if he had actually heard from God about me? I was still relatively new to this whole prophecy thing, and I wasn't sure how this worked. One thing I did know for sure was that if I was going to be able to trust that God was speaking I had to hear what I wanted to know from someone else first. I couldn't be the one to say what I was doing, so I didn't bring anything up. Draper and I made small talk at first and then he abruptly changed the conversation.

"Are you fasting?" he asked.

I couldn't believe my ears. Did he really just ask me that? Draper and I hadn't talked or seen each other in a couple weeks. He couldn't possibly have known that.

"What?" I snapped back.

"Are you fasting?"

"Well, yeah...I am fasting. Why do you ask?" I had to know. Did God tell him that or was this just some strange coincidence?

Chapter Seven PROPHETS

"I thought so. God told me you were fasting. He said you were struggling with it today." Draper said confidently.

No way. I was beside myself. Is this really happening? Did God just really answer my question? Was it really Him who called me to fast and not my own imagination? I had already started eating so I didn't expect God to speak. I figured God didn't care whether I fasted or not. I still couldn't believe my ears.

"He told you that?" I asked.

"Yep."

Draper's confidence was surprising, but I wasn't one hundred percent sure this was from God. I have more than a healthy bit of skepticism when other people tell me "God told me so." Maybe Draper had in fact seen me around town and I just didn't know it. Maybe it was coincidence. I had to know.

Having finished a few extended fasts by this point, I knew the best way to get through them was to have three things I was intentionally praying for. I always wrote down how long I was going to fast and three specific one-word topics that I was focusing my prayers on so I could keep my focus when I wanted to quit. This time they hadn't been especially helpful.

I had written down in my private prayer journal that I was praying for "anointing, clarity and breakthrough" that time. I needed to challenge Draper a little bit. This was too important to me.

"If God told you I was fasting, did He tell you for how many days?" I quizzed.

"Yep." Draper's curt responses would be something I'd get used to in the future. He enjoyed keeping the game afoot but all I could feel was anxiety.

"Well, how many?"

"21 days." I could hear Draper's smug smile through the phone. He said it with a king of swagger that you can only hear in Draper's voice.

But this wasn't good news. Draper told me exactly the number of days I would fast for, and only God and I knew that. I was in trouble because obviously I hadn't made this number up. It was important to God and here I was with popcorn grease all over my shirt.

"Did He tell you what I was fasting for?" I asked hesitantly. I figured if God had told Draper the number of days, what was the harm in asking about my requests, too?

"Yep. He told me that too."

I've never been so nervous in all my life. I wanted so badly for him to tell me my three things, but I thought I'd better not get my hopes up. That just seemed impossible. How could Draper know the things I was praying about? Could God really tell him that?

Chapter Seven **PROPHETS**

"What did He say?"

"You know," Draper sheepishly replied.

"Well, I know that I know, Draper. I want to know if you know! What did God say I was fasting for?" I wasn't going to let him off the hook.

Draper shot back, "He said you're fasting for three things: anointing, clarity and breakthrough."

The line went silent.

Draper hadn't said words similar to what I'd chosen, he said them verbatim. There's no possible way he could have guessed them; it had to have come from God. I was overwhelmed.

I don't remember how the rest of the conversation went. I'm not sure I even hung up the phone. My wife Sarah was sitting next to me the whole time soaking in the conversation. After I got off the phone I needed a moment to process what had just happened, and she wanted to know what the other half of the conversation was. It was too much for me at that moment. I just sat there stunned.

In the end I knew I'd heard directly from God, not from Draper. I determined I was going to finish the fast I'd started.

I put the bag of popcorn down, and I told the Lord that if He was good enough to speak to me like that I knew He was good enough to forgive me for doubting

Him and let me finish out my fast from there on. That word from God didn't make the rest of the fast any easier physically, but you can bet I wasn't eating another thing until my 21 days were over.

I finished that fast in awe of God's love, His voice and the level to which He cared about my life.

~ An Engaging Person ~

Sarah and I met Draper in the fall of 2003 not long after we moved to Temple, Texas. Sarah was in medical school at the time, and she ran across a guy playing a public piano in her hospital. He was worshipping the Lord beautifully in that lobby, and it caught her attention because it was so out of the ordinary. She stopped and watched as he played. Everyone else was too intimidated and a little weirded out to say anything, but Sarah went up and introduced herself briefly. She was captured by his boldness to worship God in such a public place.

We ran across him next at a church service in town a few weeks later, and he recognized Sarah and came up and said hello. I shook Draper's hand, and he immediately struck me as a little different. The whole conversation I was trying to put my finger on what made him so different. He was very engaging. You could tell instantly that he was the kind of person you'd really like to get to know. He didn't fiddle around with all the societal norms of an introductory conversation. If

Chapter Seven PROPHETS

he knew what those norms were, he didn't seem to care.

I like that in a person. I like it a lot in fact. Most of the time I play by the rules. It takes much less energy that way. What I mean is we don't really tell someone how we're feeling when we're asked. We say something like, "I'm okay." But we're never "okay." No one is. There's always something going on in our lives, but we choose to say nothing because that's how the game is played.

We also don't ask probing questions. We scratch the surface with pleasantries, especially when we meet someone new. Not Draper. After one meeting you were going to love or hate him, but you weren't going to leave without the opportunity to get to truly know him.

I get tired of playing by the rules sometimes, and I break rank. Most other people do it from time to time as well, but Draper had already thrown the rule book away. He was bold, engaging and able to instantly connect with people. From his "GQ" appearance and manner I assumed he must have been a politician or at least an aspiring one. I figured he must have an agenda to be that captivating a person.

That day we exchanged phone numbers and did the normal "let's get together" thing. At least I did. Not Draper. He insisted several times he was going to call. Almost uncomfortably so.

I got busy and went about the rest of my day and forgot about Draper until later that evening when I got a call from him.

In Draper's unique style we dispensed with our pleasantries very quickly, and I told him it had been great to meet him that morning. We chatted for a while about what each other was doing in life and just before I got off the phone he stopped me.

"I called because I needed to tell you something the Lord told me about you," Draper said boldly. "He told me He's going to give you 'double for your trouble.'"

"Double for my trouble?" I asked.

"Yep, double for your trouble."

That was vague and odd. Don't get me wrong, if God is going to promise me double for my trouble, I'll take it. What was odd was his confidence in saying it and his lack of knowing anything about me. Draper didn't know what Sarah and I had sacrificed to serve the Lord the way we were at the time. Draper didn't know all the things we'd done and all the things we'd said "no" to in the past year in trying to be obedient to God.

"What do you mean?" I shot back.

"He sees all that you've done and how hard you've worked. He sees what you've given up and He's going to give you double," Draper reassured me.

What Draper didn't know was that I had long prayed something to God from the life of Elijah and Elisha. Elijah promised that if God let Elisha see him being taken up to heaven that God would give Elisha a double portion of Elijah's anointing. I had long asked God for the same thing. If it was available to me, I wanted a double portion of God's anointing.

I had no idea what that would look like, but it seemed like something good and bold to ask for.

~ Healthy Skepticism ~

I have had lots of well-meaning people along the way promise me all kinds of things by the word of the Lord that I know weren't really God. Their heart was in the right place, and I always appreciate people trying to hear God on my behalf, but most of the time promises like that are empty. Most of the time I politely encourage them and think no more about it. I chose not to latch on to Draper's word too closely because it seemed like flattery. It was strangely close to something that was very meaningful to me, but it just seemed like someone trying to puff me up. But it did stick with me. I couldn't stop thinking about it.

It might have been the fact that a month earlier I had been praying and felt impressed by God to ask Him to release prophets in our area. This was a stirring in my heart more powerful than I'd ever felt before. It was so strong, in fact, that I felt like God wanted me to get up in front of our little home group that evening and proclaim with certainty that He was going to raise up prophets in the area, and He wanted us to pray for them.

I had never "proclaimed" anything before. Certainly not that God was going to raise up prophets. But I did it. I stood up that evening in a little small group of the leaders of our prayer ministry and proclaimed that God was raising up prophets, and we needed to join in prayer to see God do it. Needless to say that was an awkward moment.

From that day on I was really paying attention. I listened carefully to anyone who seemed to have a word from God or even looked like what I thought a prophet would look like. Until that night on the phone, Draper was neither of those things. He didn't talk like what I thought a prophet would talk like and he certainly didn't look like one.

I figured a prophet would look like John the Baptist; someone dressed like they missed the fashion memo from one hundred years ago. I expected some disheveled hobo who glared through his one good eye to speak the oracles of God to me. Draper could have been on the cover of a men's fashion magazine and he was a jock. I thought for sure no prophet could be good at sports.

That night something he said or the way he said it caused me to question all that. Could Draper truly be prophetic? The word seemed like pure flattery but something about it just wouldn't leave me.

It was a few weeks after that initial phone conversation that Draper would catch me eating popcorn.

~ THE BEGINNING OF SOMETHING NEW ~

That was the beginning of something fascinating that I never grow tired of thinking about. It may be hard to believe, but for the next four years Draper called me within the first three days of every fast I went on. During that time I went on six extended fasts, and Draper called me every time. Without fail.

He would call me and tell me how many days I was fasting for and the three things, word for word, that I was focusing on. For four years Draper didn't miss one. In fact, the last two times it happened I waited for Draper's phone call I was so sure it would happen.

God didn't disappoint.

Every single time God spoke through Draper how important those fasts were to Him. He reinforced that it wasn't just my imagination that caused me to go on these extended fasts; it was God Himself. I lived in such awe of God's love and grace to speak to me and encourage me to finish the fasts. I knew they were important, I just didn't fully know why.

I wasn't disappointed until I finally got the point. After four years I finally understood that when I felt the need to go on an extended fast it was because God was giving me grace to do it. I never heard an angel or saw some sign in the heavens. I just felt a little stirring in my heart that I needed to dedicate my heart to fast for a season for some purpose. I never even felt God give me my "three things," I always chose them myself.

After four years I understood that it was definitely God who asked me to fast. I haven't doubted since then that it was God who called me to fast, and it was then that Draper stopped calling when I fasted. The Lord no longer told him what I needed to hear because I finally believed it for myself. From that point on I haven't heard from Draper during a fast. I no longer doubt that when I feel like I should fast it's from God. My wife certainly does, but I don't.

I've got many more "Draper Stories" to tell. Draper has called me and told me what I prayed and the Lord's answer to that prayer 40 times or more since then. Often Draper tells me word-for-word what I pray or write down in secret. Nothing is hidden from the God who speaks into prophets' ears, and I love it when God speaks those things to me. Draper has given me encouragement and chastisement from God, and I love them both the same.

Whether God tells me He likes what I'm doing or when He steadies my hand from sin, I love hearing from Him. Both are for my good, and I know God speaks both because of His great love for me.

Many people are afraid of hearing from God because they think He'll expose their sin, but they've not considered the true nature of their sin. All our unconfessed sin lies open and bare before the God of heaven. He knows anyway, so it's always for our good to hear from God to repent. I've needed that many times in my life, and God has been so kind and faithful to use Draper for me in that way.

I know for sure beyond a shadow of a doubt that I'm God's son because He's corrected me. It's never pleasant, but I always love God for it. He cares enough about me to bring me back onto the right path.

Chapter Prayer

Lord, will You release prophets in my church, city, state and region, so that Your Holy Church will reflect Your glory, love and power?

Chapter Eight

JESUS, A HOT DOG AND A COKE

It was a hot summer, which didn't help my work ethic. I was working for a company that to this day I still love the people there more than any place I've ever worked. The management was great, and my co-workers were awesome. I was just mostly bored by the job. I was not doing the best I could, but no one could really tell because most of them liked me pretty well.

I was giving the job less than my all, though, and even if no one else knew it, I did. The Lord had already dealt with me once about giving my job less than my all, and I found myself back in the same position again. This time around, my company was in a hiring frenzy, and I was tasked with helping to interview a lot of candidates. The interviews had run their course for the most part, and things were starting to wind down,

Chapter Eight **JESUS, A HOT DOG AND A COKE**

which I was happy about. It meant no more extra work.

A week or so after what I was sure was the last interview, I made plans to leave the office early, around four o'clock, to meet my wife for an early date. We were going out to eat, which was somewhat rare at the time with her busy schedule. I was excited about getting some quality time with Sarah when I got a call on my cell phone from an old friend.

~ DRAPER SMITH ~

"Hey Draper, how are you?" I asked.

"Good, man. I'm calling because I had a crazy dream about you last night," Draper quickly replied.

I knew what that meant when Draper felt like calling me the next day after a dream. It meant it was important. I asked him to tell me what happened.

Draper said that in his dream, Jesus, he and I were sitting at a Little League baseball game, sitting in the bleachers eating a hot dog and drinking Cokes. We were watching the game and having a good time. Draper said the seating arrangement was Jesus, Draper and Darren.

"How come you always get to sit next to Jesus?" I kidded with him.

Draper chuckled and continued. "We were having a great time and then Jesus looked at me and said, 'Darren has been hiring people at work, and he's not taking it seriously. Tell him to take it seriously.'"

~Reading My Mail~

I was stunned. Draper, who lived a few hundred miles away and certainly wasn't privy to my inner thought life, read me like a book. In a dream, the Lord had told him exactly what had been going on with me at my job. I was instantly crushed. I told Draper that he was exactly right. Even though the "hiring" wasn't totally up to me, I had been involved in many interviews and I wasn't taking it as seriously as I knew I should have —certainly not as seriously as Jesus wanted me to.

I repented and silently told the Lord I was sorry for being so disobedient.

Draper acted like that was the end of the dream, but he quickly chimed in. "Oh, and one more thing. The Lord told me that He would give you one more opportunity today at 5:37."

"That is oddly specific," I thought to myself, then I remembered my date with Sarah that evening. "Draper, you really did hear from the Lord, but I think you might have missed it on that part. I won't be here today at 5:37. I'm going on a date with Sarah," was my sure reply.

Chapter Eight JESUS, A HOT DOG AND A COKE

~ NOT BACKING DOWN ~

Draper was unapologetic and unmoving about the date and time. He was one hundred percent convinced that the Lord was going to let me have another shot at it that day and at that time, not another day. I tried to help him out a little and say he had heard wrong. Maybe it would happen tomorrow—but he would have none of it.

I've had many exchanges with Draper like this through the years. It is hard to put it in words the banter we've gone back and forth with, but it's a happy part of our friendship in the Lord for me. I'm glad he didn't back off of what the Lord showed him even with my insistence. We're both pretty obstinate, but I believe so in good ways.

One thing was for sure: I was not going to cancel my date just because a "prophet" told me to do so. I have seen far too many people in the charismatic church fall lockstep in line with something someone said and change their entire lives just because the person who said it claimed to be a prophet. I knew Draper was a prophet, but still I wasn't about to do that. Even he can be wrong (although I can't put my finger on a time that he has been). I know that I do not have to be intimidated by a prophet or prophetic word. I know that if my heart is constantly moving toward the Lord in an attitude of prayer, the Lord wins those situations. This was one such occasion.

~ God Wins ~

I thanked Draper for being open to hear the Lord on my behalf, and I hung up, fully believing that he was wrong about the date and time. I did leave at 4:00 pm that day, but I only got ten minutes away from the office when my phone rang. Our secretary called me to tell me that both of my bosses were in a meeting they couldn't get out of, and they asked if I could come back and do an interview they forgot was coming in that day. It would have been enough to get me turned around that the people who rubber stamp my paycheck asked me to come back, but I knew I had been set up by the Lord that day. I knew I couldn't say no.

I turned my car around and rushed back to the office. I sat down and started the interview, going through our normal process and questions, but this time I was very focused. The entire time I was asking the Lord what he thought, paying attention not only to what the interviewee was saying, but also the subtle voice of the Holy Spirit. Eventually, my boss came in and helped me finish the interview. After it was over, he walked the interviewee out of the office, since it was now after hours, and I stared out the window pondering what had happened that day.

The man had answered all the questions the way we would like, but I kept feeling like the Lord said "no." My boss walked back into the office and immediately asked me, "Well, what do you think?"

Chapter Eight JESUS, A HOT DOG AND A COKE

I looked down at my watch. It couldn't be.

5:37 pm

Draper wasn't a minute off. I'm not speechless very often, but in that moment I didn't have an answer for my boss. I'm sure he thought I was a buffoon, but I was at a complete loss for words. I eventually stumbled out a "no" to his surprise. He thought the guy was great, but I knew the Lord had said no. Because I said no, my boss decided not to hire the man.

~ LISTENING TO THE LORD ~

I don't know why the Lord said no. I'm sure the man wasn't some kind of horrible axe-murderer or something, but my guess is that the Lord, who sees everything, knew he wouldn't be a good fit for the company. How many times, you people who hire others, wish you could know that on the front end?

That experience is logged away in my heart as one of the most cherished rebukes and supernatural prophetic experiences of my life. I always try to ask the Lord what He is thinking about things like that now. The Lord really cares about our businesses, not just because He sees them as evangelism opportunities or paychecks to support the "truly important" work of the church, but because the actual work we do matters to Him.

I have had several prophetic rebukes from the Lord like this one, and in every case I can remember the Lord has always appeared to me as a friend. This time it was having fun at a baseball game. I love that even God's rebukes are always meant for our good. I trust and ask the Lord for rebukes when I need them and can't see it myself, because He is always so good and kind to me.

Have you ever been rebuked by the Lord? Was He kind? Was He a friend?

Have you ever taken your job less seriously than you should because you don't feel like it is the true "work of ministry?" I tell you, Jesus cares about your job, your company and your work. Not because of what it will do for the church, but because His church is where you are working.

Chapter Prayer

Lord, show me the value of my work. Will You please speak to me about my daily tasks, projects, co-workers and overseers. I want to bring your kingdom to my workplace.

Chapter Nine
THE MOST HELPFUL GIFT

I first started asking for dreams after an encounter with a prophet named Paul Cain. He spoke at a church in Houston, Texas in 1995, and my good friend David May invited me to hear him. He neglected to tell me at the time that he was a "prophet." I would not have gone had I known that.

I was shocked to find out the church we were at was very charismatic, something I was not comfortable with at all. The worship, dancing, flags and emotional response of those in attendance caused me great distress, so I was very happy when worship was over.

I was to be greeted with more distress when Mr. Cain took the stage. He spent an eternity telling bad church jokes and occasionally mumbling about something I had never heard before. He kept saying, "I'm just waiting for the anointing."

Chapter Nine THE MOST HELPFUL GIFT

~ THE ANOINTING ~

That was a strange phrase to me. I had never once heard it before in church, so I wasn't sure what exactly he was waiting for. After each new joke he would repeat that line and I would be puzzled again, but not long enough to tame my boredom with the service and his jokes.

Halfway through the fifth "A Methodist, Presbyterian and Baptist walk into a bar" joke something changed dramatically. He abruptly stopped telling the joke and, in a voice that sounded like something from a 1950's tent revival, began to proclaim loudly and emphatically what the Lord was doing.

"This is going to be a year of brokenness!" He shouted. He continued, "That doesn't always come with tears, but there will be many tears this year as the Lord breaks our hearts."

As soon as he said the word "tears" three women in different parts of the room began wailing. I had never heard anything like that before and have never since heard anything like it except for my experience in Guatemala where the mother wept for her dead three-year-old. I was instantly shocked by the sound of the wailing, and I couldn't stop the thoughts that ran through my mind.

"They have to be faking it."

It was not long before more and more people were wailing around the room. I do not remember anything else Mr. Cain said that evening, but I do remember what happened to me. As soon as the weeping started, I felt something I had never felt before and haven't since.

At the same moment the women began weeping something hit me that felt like a wave as if I was at the beach jumping through the breakers. It hit me and moved me back ever so slightly like I was used to at the beach I grew up at. I knew I had not faked it, and I knew I had not asked for it, so I was puzzled. "What hit me?" I pondered.

As I was trying to reconcile what happened to me and my skepticism about the wailing women in the room, the woman sitting next to me quickly fell to the floor and starting wailing. I looked at her face and how her body was contorting and thought to myself, "Woah. She's not faking."

~ FIGURING THINGS OUT ~

I left that meeting not knowing what to make of the whole experience. I did not believe the Lord still did such things, but I had experienced something firsthand that I could not define.

Over the next few months I read, pondered and prayed about what I had experienced. I asked the Lord

Chapter Nine THE MOST HELPFUL GIFT

if all this charismatic stuff I had been taught to believe was "the devil"–wasn't actually really Him. The same friend who drug me along to the Paul Cain event invited me to come to a church he had been playing guitar at, called Calvary Baptist Church in Houston, Texas.

One day, a few months after the Paul Cain encounter, I was at Calvary early because my friend David was practicing with the worship team. As I sat in the empty rows of chairs I read 1 Corinthians 12-14 where Paul speaks about spiritual gifts, love and the supremacy of prophecy. I closed my Bible and uttered a quick question to God, "If You still do this stuff, would you show me?"

Very shortly after that people began filing in and the service started. I was beginning to enjoy the worship style that Calvary embraced, and I felt more comfortable in a "charismatic" church than I did months before. I was about to feel much more comfortable.

When worship ended, Calvary's pastor, Steve Meeks, took the stage and immediately asked everyone to turn to 1 Corinthians 12. My jaw dropped. He read from the same passages I was meditating on and in a very clear way answered my questions on the Lord's behalf. The answer was a resounding "yes!"

That may not seem like a sure answer to such an important fleece, but to my young heart it was enough. That gave me the license to pray for the Lord to speak to me. I made a point to ask the Lord every day to speak to me prophetically, and over the next five years I do not remember forgetting to ask too many days. For five years, however, I do not remember hearing anything significant. That is, until my trip to Guatemala. That was when things started for me.

~ Pray for Prophecy ~

In no uncertain terms, Paul tells us we should all seek the spiritual gift of prophecy. In 1 Corinthians 14 he tells us it is, above all, the most helpful gift God gives to the church. Why wouldn't it be? What could be more helpful than God speaking directly to us?

> *¹Follow the way of love and eagerly desire gifts of the Spirit, especially prophecy. ²For anyone who speaks in a tongue does not speak to people but to God. Indeed, no one understands them; they utter mysteries by the Spirit. ³But the one who prophesies speaks to people for their strengthening, encouraging and comfort. ⁴Anyone who speaks in a tongue edifies themselves, but the one who prophesies edifies the church. ⁵I would like every one of you to speak in tongues,but I would rather have you prophesy. The one who prophesies is greater than the one who speaks in tongues,unless someone interprets, so that the church may be edified.*
>
> *1 Corinthians 14:1-5*

Chapter Nine THE MOST HELPFUL GIFT

At first glance this may not make much sense, but in context it means all the world to us. Paul introduces the spiritual gifts in 1 Corinthians 12, then in chapter 13 he tells us that without love nothing we receive from God is worthwhile. He concludes this line of thinking with the passage above about the supremacy of prophecy.

There is no gift so helpful to the church as prophecy. Whereas we should eagerly desire all spiritual gifts, we should pay special attention to seek God to speak directly to us. When God speaks directly to us, it invigorates our hearts, challenges us with the reality of the supernatural and reminds us of the imminence of eternity. Prophecy, when used properly and in order in church, will keep us on the straight path God has for us. Without that prophetic vision, we are quick to wander astray.

~ Some Ground Rules ~

Paul is quick to transition to some ground rules on the use of tongues and prophecy in worship meetings in 1 Corinthians 14 because when misused or abused, prophecy becomes not only unhelpful, but deadly. He tells us that all things we do in our worship services should be done in order.

> ^{29}*Two or three prophets should speak, and the others should weigh carefully what is said. ^{30}And if a revelation comes to someone who is*

> *sitting down, the first speaker should stop. ³¹For you can all prophesy in turn so that everyone may be instructed and encouraged. ³²The spirits of prophets are subject to the control of prophets. ³³For God is not a God of disorder but of peace—as in all the congregations of the Lord's people.*
>
> 1 Corinthians 14:29-33

It is interesting that Paul would put constraints on prophecy the same as he does for tongues just before this passage. If prophecy is God speaking, why would there need to be rules? Cannot God just speak as He wills when and where He pleases during a church service?

I have personally seen that mentality play out in church services, and I can wholeheartedly agree with Paul in his restrictions. The problem we have is not with God speaking, but that He chooses to do it through people. It is the human element that Paul is addressing and trying to bring some order to. If the Lord speaks to us, we will always struggle to share that with others through the filter of our humanity.

Then there are the people who believe the Lord has spoken to them when in fact He has not. Others must constantly judge words from prophecies when given to discern whether or not the Lord is speaking or if it is just the good-natured heart of the person delivering the word. When you think about all the ways in which this can go wrong, it is easy to see the mess that can take place.

That is why we need ground rules for prophecy. Prophecy is messy. We may hear from the Lord and misunderstand it. We may think we have heard from God when we did not. We may declare what God wanted kept private, and we sometimes hold on to things God wants shared. That is the nature of people: we are prone to mess these things up.

One of the most important ground rules for prophecy is that subjective prophetic words can never be viewed as equal to, or superseding the objective, written Word of God. Because we must view everything God says to us today through the filter of human subjectivity, it is a most dangerous proposition to view a man's words today with equal standing to scripture.

Let me make this clear: do not ever hold subjective prophetic words as anything but completely submissive and subjugated to the written Word of God.

~ Grace And Love ~

We must consider in what context Paul is sharing these things. One chapter before these prophetic regulations, Paul gave us 1 Corinthians 13, potentially one of his more famous chapters, colloquially known as the "love chapter."

I have seen churches that display great grace and love toward people in all of their dealings until a prophetic person tries to speak, then they become cold and mean. They distrust the person and submit them to the most rigorous and stringent tests imaginable, mostly hoping for them to fail in their stand for God.

I have also seen churches that will accept at face value anything a person says under the hospices of "prophecy." This is true especially for traveling prophetic ministers. Churches accept and implement whatever a prophetic person says with no care or concern to discerning whether the Lord is speaking.

Both of these situations are error. We must be diligent to discern prophetic words, because subjective information from God is inherently messy. We must also remember that it is always people delivering this message. People need grace. People need love. People need friends and co-laborers to walk alongside them and help them grow. The idea of iron sharpening iron (Proverbs 27:17) applies equally to prophetic ministry the same as it does anything else.

Most often excesses in either direction are caused by intimidation of the prophetic ministry. I have seen overreactions at either end of the spectrum because pastors, leaders and people are afraid of prophecy. "Will God expose my sins?" some think. "Will God disappoint me when something doesn't come true? Will God be mad at me for opposing a prophetic

Chapter Nine THE MOST HELPFUL GIFT

word?" These kinds of thoughts are very real and very powerful factors in churches experiencing the freedom and benefit of prophetic ministry.

Our foundation must always be in the confidence that comes from our freedom in Jesus. Pastors, leaders and congregations need not fear God in prophetic words because He is always good. That must be our foundation: God is always good. When we believe that, we may open ourselves up to whatever God may have for us.

Does he rebuke us sometimes? Yes, He does. Does God expose our secret sins through prophetic ministry? He absolutely can! Does He ever have any intention but the best for us when He does such things? Of course not!

God only does things to us and through us to benefit us. Consider the words He spoke to Jeremiah:

> *"For I know the plans I have for you," declares the LORD, "plans to prosper you and not to harm you, plans to give you hope and a future."*
>
> *Jeremiah 29:11*

God only wants the best for our lives, and He will use whatever means He feels necessary to accomplish that end in us. I have been personally rebuked and exposed in sin before by prophetic people, and whereas it is never pleasant, I am always thankful that the Lord loves me enough to speak even to the weakest places of my life.

~ A Seat At The Table ~

Pastoring churches can be hard. There are always so many problems, so many concerns that pastors must carry for the people they are trying to lead. Add to that the need for strategic direction so the church can grow, and you can quickly see how pastors carry a burden far too heavy for them to bear alone.

Allowing God to have a "seat at our table" of leadership in the church is one of the most beneficial things pastors can do for their church. What would be better than to allow God the ability to speak into the circumstances of leadership we most need Him for? Does God not have opinions about how our churches should run? Do you think He cares about how we minister, how we grow our churches and how we deal with problems?

I have personally experienced the Lord's leading hand through prophetic words as well as His corrective hand when I have made the wrong decision. Both are critical. In church leadership, we need marching orders and we need reprimands when we go the wrong direction on our own, which we most certainly will. God is good enough to give us both if we let Him.

Chapter Nine THE MOST HELPFUL GIFT

Definitely seek God for healing in your church. Make a point to allow God the room to give tongues, miracles, signs and wonders. You will be glad you did if you are prepared to steward it. But above all, make room for God to speak prophetically. Paul is correct in 1 Corinthians 14:1 in saying that we should "eagerly desire gifts of the Spirit, especially prophecy."

There is no gift so helpful to the life, growth and health of the church than the gift of God speaking directly to us. What better way do we have to know what God would want us to do than for Him just to tell us?

Chapter Prayer

Lord, speak to my church prophetically. My church desperately needs to know what You think about what we are doing and how we can follow You with more passion. Make a humble people who will listen to You where I am today, and give us the character to discern Your voice.

A Sample Chapter from

THE YEAR OF THE LORD'S FAVOR?

Chapter 6
Now The Good News

Available Today at Amazon.com

NOW THE GOOD NEWS

The gospel of Jesus Christ does not actually become "good" news without a healthy understanding of the bad news that precedes it. If we do not understand that we are sinners justly condemned to an eternity of punishment and separation from God, then the news of Jesus' sacrifice is just, well, news.

News becomes good news when it is contrasted with something that looks worse. When I was in college I called up my parents after one semester and told them that I had failed three classes, gotten arrested and was being considered for expulsion. When they got over the initial shock, I told them I had made a D in one class. The initial shock (even though they did not buy it) sure made the truth seem a lot better.

The difference in America's situation is that the bad news is real. There is no fabrication needed when we look at scripture and history. God will judge a wicked and rebellious nation that is filled with innocent blood, corruption and repression. Our bad news is very real. Our good news is also very real, but we must choose to accept it.

The good news in our situation is that America does not have to continue to go the wrong way. The great news in our situation, I believe, is that we do not even have to change any laws or lobby for policy change. The good news will come as a result of repentance on the part of God's people.

~ The Power of Repentance ~

If we repent, God may just relent from His righteous judgment over our nation.

> *If my people, who are called by my name, will humble themselves and pray and seek my face and turn from their wicked ways, then will I hear from heaven and will forgive their sin and will heal their land.*
>
> *2 Chronicles 7:14*

The key part of this verse is "my people." God is not requiring us to legislate morality on the part of the lost in our nation. He is requiring "His people" to repent. If God's people will repent of our wicked ways, then God will turn aside from His judgment and heal our land. He will leave a blessing instead of a curse.

> [12]*"Now, therefore," says the Lord, "Turn to Me with all your heart, with fasting, with weeping, and with mourning." *[13]*So rend your heart, and*

> *not your garments; Return to the Lord your God, For He is gracious and merciful, Slow to anger, and of great kindness; And He relents from doing harm.*
>
> *¹⁴Who knows if He will turn and relent, And leave a blessing behind Him—A grain offering and a drink offering For the Lord your God?*
>
> *¹⁵Blow the trumpet in Zion, Consecrate a fast, Call a sacred assembly;*
>
> *¹⁶Gather the people, Sanctify the congregation, Assemble the elders, Gather the children and nursing babes; Let the bridegroom go out from his chamber, And the bride from her dressing room.*
>
> Joel 2:12-16

The good news in America's situation is there is still time for God to leave a blessing instead of a curse. God is gracious and compassionate, slow to anger and abounding in love. Moses' statement is very important for us today:

> *¹⁸'The LORD is slow to anger and abundant in lovingkindness, forgiving iniquity and transgression; but He will by no means clear the guilty, visiting the iniquity of the fathers on the children to the third and the fourth generations.'*
>
> *¹⁹"Pardon, I pray, the iniquity of this people according to the greatness of Your lovingkindness,*

> *just as You also have forgiven this people, from Egypt even until now."*
>
> *Numbers 14:18-19*

God will not leave the guilty unpunished, but He is patient. He is slow to anger. God is longing to release a blessing over America, but He will only do it on His terms.

We in America have become so familiar with the "grace of God" message that we often forget the very nature of our relationship to Him. We must remember that we are the created and He is the creator. We do not make the rules. We do not get to bend them. We can only play by God's set of rules. Paul says it well in Romans:

> *Therefore consider the goodness and severity of God: on those who fell, severity; but toward you, goodness, if you continue in His goodness. Otherwise you also will be cut off.*
>
> *Romans 11:22*

~ God's Grace ~

We must realize that God longs to be gracious to us, but He requires that we do things His way. We do not get to live however we want and expect God to bless us. His grace is not bestowed upon us without adherence to His ways. It is a confusing concept for many in the church today. For many, the question is, "Is God's grace free or are there requirements we must meet to receive it?"

The answer is both, from our perspective. We cannot do anything to earn God's grace. It is very much a free gift, but at the same time, we must repent, change our lives and strive to live according to God's ways. Our reality seems quite paradoxical. This has been the challenge of theologians for centuries trying to understand this.

There is nothing we can do to earn God's grace, but He does tell us plainly that we must play by His rules if we want to walk in it. That is true on a personal level as well as a societal (corporate) level.

We must not be so foolish to think that our nation will continue to receive God's grace and blessing if we choose to live contrary to how God requires. We cannot claim God but live contrary to who He is. If we do return to Him "with all our hearts" He may just leave a blessing behind. We certainly do not deserve a blessing just for repenting, but that is where God's grace is free. We cannot earn it, but if we choose to obey Him He will grant it to us.

America's greatest days may still be ahead, but it will take resolve on the part of God's people, the church. At this point in time I believe we have two vastly different possible outcomes. One outcome will be the result of changing nothing; the other will be a result of changing everything.

So what will repentance look like? What must the church do to receive this blessing from God? What are the practical steps we must take to see God relent from His anger over our nation and the injustices we have perpetrated?

~ Personal Repentance ~

What is at stake in America is not really personal judgment but corporate judgment. Individually, we will all stand before the Lord one day and face judgment. If we believe in Jesus, we will be judged righteous and enter into eternity with God. Then our actions here on earth will be judged and we will be rewarded accordingly.

America will not stand before God on the day of Judgment. It stands for its judgment now and America will rise and fall based on how it responds to the challenges it faces today. But America is not just a flag or a bald eagle on a quarter. It is made up of people. Millions of them. America's outcome before the court of heaven depends on how individuals respond.

That brings us to personal repentance. America cannot repent corporately without individual repentance. The nation must have leaders humble enough to take the first step to bow low before the Lord. By leaders, I do not mean the president and congress. I mean people who are willing to take the lead in repenting themselves and calling others to repentance.

Pastors, teachers, plumbers, engineers, writers, attorneys, carpenters, doctors, janitors, secretaries, CEOs and electricians can all be the leaders we need to take that first step. We can be so paralyzed by fear of stepping out, hoping that a true leader will emerge, that we never take that first step.

God is not asking for leaders to take the first step toward leading this nation down the right path, but He is asking for anyone to lead who is willing. Look at what scripture says:

> *26Brothers and sisters, think of what you were when you were called. Not many of you were wise by human standards; not many were influential; not many were of noble birth. 27But God chose the foolish things of the world to shame the wise; God chose the weak things of the world to shame the strong. 28God chose the lowly things of this world and the despised things—and the things that are not—to nullify the things that are, 29so that no one may boast before him. 30It is because of him that you are in Christ Jesus, who has become for us wisdom from God—that is, our righteousness, holiness and redemption.*
>
> *1 Corinthians 1:26-30*

God has not chosen the wise, the rich or the powerful to lead His kingdom. He has chosen those He knows will say yes. He has chosen those with a humble heart who know it is not their own abilities but God's that makes the difference. God is not looking for influential people to change our nation, but for humble people who will rely on His influence to change us.

That all starts with our own personal willingness to repent. Will we choose to follow God with all our hearts before we try or expect anyone else to?

Are you trapped in pornography? Greed? Theft? Gambling? Drugs and alcohol? Abuse? Self-righteousness? Living for yourself? Go to God and ask for help. Repent of your sin and ask Him for help to overcome them. Make restitution for the things you have stolen from others and do what you need to restore relationships.

Zacchaeus was so overwhelmed by the grace and forgiveness he experienced from Jesus that he could not think of doing anything but an extravagant act of repentance.

> *But Zacchaeus stood up and said to the Lord, "Look, Lord! Here and now I give half of my possessions to the poor, and if I have cheated anybody out of anything, I will pay back four times the amount."*
>
> *Luke 19:8*

Will you be so overcome by the reality of Jesus' forgiveness of your sins that you will humble yourself to repentance? Do you have too much to lose by admitting you have sinned? Consider the eternity that God has offered to us. This life is unthinkably short in comparison to eternity with God. Nothing else makes sense now but to live for eternity. What little respect, honor and dignity we have now will be gone in just a moment, and we will stand before a loving and righteous God. In that hour we will consider every act of repentance and humility the wisest decision of our life.

~ Corporate Repentance ~

One of the amazing things about God is how He rewards. All men and women seek honor, dignity, respect and even fame. We long for greatness. That may look different for each of us, but the longing is in us all. It is not sinful because God put it in us. He longs to reward us for eternity. He wants us great forever.

What makes that longing sinful is when we try to fulfill it with illicit desires. It is hard for us humans to rightly see eternity and change our lives now based on it, but that is what God is asking of us. We can seek our own glory and honor here on earth, but we have no power to earn glory and honor in eternity. Only God can grant that.

What is amazing is that God also has the power to give to us honor and respect in this life, too. We fight and claw our way to the "top" in this life, but it is all futility. Only God has the authority to give us respect, honor, dignity, authority and greatness in eternity *and* this age.

That means there is nothing else that makes sense for us as a nation but to humble ourselves and return to the Lord. That kind of repentance will start with the ones who choose to personally repent. It will become contagious when others see the power of God on their lives.

The power of God is not just in miracles, signs and wonders (although those are great). The true power of God as experienced by people in this life is the ability to transform us from self-seeking sinners into eternally-focused lovers of God. Miracles, signs and wonders are powerful, but nothing changes a people like the stirrings of revival.

As more and more people bow their hearts low before the Lord, they feel the cleansing power of His blood, love and forgiveness. That is a fire that spreads faster than in any forest because people are so hungry to see real change. Real love. Real joy. Real peace.

Our personal repentance will not stay personal. As we seek God's face with more and more energy, our lives will become contagious. Others will want what we have.

We need revival that can only come from God, but amazingly He only stirs hearts through partnership with us. When one person humbles himself before

God, it makes two others jealous for the same freedom. When those two humble themselves, it makes four more hungry for the same cleansing of their hearts. Then eight turn into 16 and 16 into 32 and before long you have a massive stirring of souls turning to the Lord.

Nothing spreads faster than hearts truly energized by the love and forgiveness of Jesus. That kind of revival does not take long before it affects a nation.

But it has to start with you. We cannot wait for three other people to repent and humble themselves and return to the Lord. We have to risk looking foolish. We have to risk seeming less "holy." We have to give up our right to having everyone think we are put together.

Do you want to see America repent and be blessed by God? It does not start with the president, congress or even your pastor; it starts with you.

~ Start Here ~

People are not stupid. They have seen Christians call everyone else to repentance for decades now without seeing any true change in us. We cannot fake repentance. Not before God and not even before others. The only ones we truly deceive are ourselves.

America has seen the repentance and call to righteous living we have offered them and they have issued a collective "no." Christians have almost completely lost the culture that was ours to influence because no one sees anything different in us than in themselves.

People are smart enough to spot the phony calls for morality we have given them, but they are also powerless but to acknowledge true change when they see it. America is not a stubborn nation refusing to turn to the Lord. Our nation is hungry to see God move here, but it has been decades since we have seen it.

The revival and awakening America needs will start with God's people. Are we willing to turn our calls for morality in on ourselves? Are we willing to silence our attempts to legislate others' lives and first start living wholly for God ourselves?

A simple message of hope backed by the power of God's love on our lives will transform our nation. It has changed the course of history for two thousand years, and it is still what we need today.

> *¹And so it was with me, brothers and sisters. When I came to you, I did not come with eloquence or human wisdom as I proclaimed to you the testimony about God. ²For I resolved to know nothing while I was with you except Jesus Christ and him crucified. ³I came to you in weakness with great fear and trembling. ⁴My message and my preaching were not with wise and persuasive words, but with a demonstration of the Spirit's power, ⁵so that your faith*

might not rest on human wisdom, but on God's power.

1 Corinthians 2:1-5

About The Author

Darren Hibbs has worked in industry and in full-time ministry. As a writer, he has published several books.

Darren has great passion for revival in America and longs to see the church embrace God's correction so that we may receive the fullness of what He has to offer us.

Darren's heart burns to bring a message of hope to a lost and broken world through the immeasurable love of Jesus. It is his heart that the church will grow in love for God and embrace His love and power so that the lost will see and hear the good news about Jesus as they see it change us.

Darren writes regularly and can be reached at www.DarrenHibbs.com.

OTHER BOOKS BY DARREN HIBBS

Two days before 9/11, an angel visited Darren in a dream and showed him the collapse of the World Trade Center. In another dream in 2003, the Lord showed Darren that in the days when the replacement building, One World Trade, was complete, America would hang in the balance.

Find out how these remarkable prophesies came true and what it means to you today.

Revelation: A 10 Week Bible Study is a different kind of Bible Study that will take you deep into the scriptures and cause you to engage God's Word like never before.

With helpful commentary and probing questions, the 10 Week Bible study will help you find a new love for God's Word. Ten weeks really can change your life!

BOTH ARE AVAILABLE AT AMAZON.COM TODAY

www.ingramcontent.com/pod-product-compliance
Lightning Source LLC
Chambersburg PA
CBHW071707040426
42446CB00011B/1951